HAPKIDO

합기도

HAPKIDO

AN INTRODUCTION TO THE ART OF SELF-DEFENSE

MARC TEDESCHI

Floating World Editions

Hapkido: An Introduction to the Art of Self-Defense

Copyright © 2000 by Marc Tedeschi

Originally published May 2001 in a high-quality
softcover edition by Weatherhill, Inc.,
an imprint of Shambhala Publications, Inc.
This softcover edition published May 2015
by Floating World Editions, Inc.

FIRST EDITION, 2001
Third Printing, 2006
Floating World Edition, 2015

Book and cover design: Marc Tedeschi
Photography: Shelley Firth, Frank Deras
Creative consultant: Michele Wetherbee
Editorial supervision: Thomas Tedeschi, Ray Furse
Other acknowledgments are found on the last page.

Library of Congress Cataloging-in-Publication Data
(for the previous edition of this book)
Tedeschi, Marc.
  Hapkido: an introduction to the art of
  self-defense / Marc Tedeschi. —1st ed.
      p. cm.
  Includes bibliographical references.
  ISBN 0-8348-0483-2
  1. Hapkido. I. Title
GV1114.39 .T42 2001
796.815'3—dc21   2001026091

Notice of Liability
The information in this book is distributed without
warranty and is only presented as a means of
preserving a unique aspect of the heritage of the
martial arts. All information and techniques are to
be used at the reader's sole discretion. While every
precaution has been taken in preparation of this
book, neither the author nor publisher shall have
any liability to any person or entity with respect
to injury, loss, or damage caused or alleged to
be caused directly or indirectly by the contents
contained in this book or by the procedures or
processes described herein. There is no guarantee
that the techniques described or shown in this book
will be safe or effective in any self-defense or
medical situation, or otherwise. You may be injured
if you apply or train in the techniques described in
this book. Consult a physician regarding whether
to attempt any technique described in this book.
Specific self-defense responses illustrated in this
book may not be justified in any particular situation
in view of all of the circumstances or under the
applicable federal, state, or local laws.

Trademarks:
Kuk Sool Won™ and Hwa Rang Do® are claimed
as trademarks of their respective owners.

—
FOR SHELLEY
—

This book is intended to provide readers
with a brief overview of Hapkido,
a comprehensive and immensely varied
martial art of self-defense, and to give
novice students essential guidance during
their first several months of training.
Readers seeking a comprehensive
presentation of the art should
consult the author's 1136-page work,
Hapkido: Traditions, Philosophy, Technique,
which is shown above (ISBN 0-8348-0444-1).
For further information, please visit
www.marctedeschi.com

CONTENTS

How This Book is Organized

To help the reader comprehend the vast amount of material that defines Hapkido, this book is organized into five parts:

Part 1 is a brief overview of history, philosophy, and technique.

Part 2 is a brief overview of some of the more important basic technical elements that define Hapkido.

Part 3 shows how basic skills are combined for practical self-defense. Sixty techniques are shown in detail. They are a representative sample drawn from thousands of Hapkido techniques.

Part 4 is a very brief overview of Hapkido weapon systems and shows 11 typical techniques. They are a representative sample drawn from over 470 common Hapkido techniques.

Reference material includes information on rank advancement, important Korean terms, and sources for further reading.

Editorial Notes

The following editorial conventions have been adopted for use in this book: To avoid sexist grammar, *they*, *them*, *their*, and *themselves* are used in place of the singular pronouns *he*, *she*, *him*, *her*, *his*, *hers*, *himself*, and *herself*. To avoid wordiness, articles are sometimes omitted from captions and technical descriptions, and abbreviations are employed, specifically: (R) for right, (L) for left, (cw) for clockwise, and (ccw) for counterclockwise. Personal names are written English-language style, given name followed by surname.

PART 1

INTRODUCTION

Overview

Since its beginnings in the mid-twentieth century, Hapkido has been primarily an oral tradition. The few books that have been published over the years are quite limited in scope, no doubt hampered by the enormity of the task involved in organizing, structuring, and explaining a martial art composed of thousands of techniques. This lack of literature has led to widespread misunderstanding about exactly what Hapkido is, and is not.

In October 2000, the most definitive work ever written on Hapkido was published under the title, *Hapkido: Traditions, Philosophy, Technique.* This 1136-page work contains more than 9000 photographs, documents over 2000 martial techniques, and has been acclaimed to be the most comprehensive martial arts text ever written. Nonetheless, not everyone needs, wants, or can afford such a substantial book on the subject. Consequently, this smaller introductory book has been written by the same author, to provide a brief overview of Hapkido, and to give novice students basic material to assist them during their initial months of training.

Although this book has been based on its 1136-page predecessor, it is important to recognize that no book consisting of several hundred pages can ever hope to accurately document Hapkido in its entirety. Please do not believe that by studying the techniques in this book you have mastered the art. This is not possible. To study a martial art in a serious and responsible manner means to study it in its entirety—its history, philosophy, and technique. Some aspects of Hapkido can be learned from a book; however, there is much that can only be learned by direct experience, and by training for years under a qualified master. A quality book can amplify this process, but it cannot replace it. Serious martial artists seeking a more comprehensive understanding of Hapkido are urged to buy the larger work, on which this book is based, and to train in a serious, dedicated, and joyful manner. For in the end, it is the quality and frequency of one's training that matters most.

What is Hapkido?

Hapkido is a Korean martial art which emerged in the mid-twentieth century and quickly grew to become an international style. Its founders created the art by selectively fusing a wide range of existing martial skills, with new innovations. As a result, Hapkido possesses one of the most complex, unique, and varied arsenals of self-defense techniques to be found in any martial art. These techniques encompass all major martial categories: strikes, kicks, blocks, avoiding movements, holds, joint locks, chokes, throws, breakfalls, tumbling, ground fighting, weapons, meditation, and healing.

Like many Asian martial arts, Hapkido emphasizes the unification of body, mind, and spirit; the perfection of human character; social responsibility; and appropriate use of force. Unlike most martial arts, Hapkido utilizes more than 1100 core techniques, which are intuitively modified or combined to create thousands of variations. Self-defense techniques are characterized by a constant flow of striking, blocking, holding, and throwing techniques. Constant motion and fluid circular movements are designed to blend with an opponent's force. Tactics often alternate between highly aggressive and defensive modes, with power being generated through use of one's entire body. Internal energy development is fundamental to all training, leading to increased health and greater efficiency in self-defense techniques.

Hapkido techniques are not only for self-defense. Meditation and healing techniques are used to develop emotional stability, peace of mind, and confidence, while providing the same health benefits found in other arts, such as Tai Chi Chuan and Qi Gong. Thus, Hapkido is a highly practical self-defense art with strong spiritual underpinnings.

In contemporary society, Hapkido is mostly practiced for self-defense, health, and spiritual growth. Although it is often compared to Aikido, Taekwondo, Jujutsu, Judo, and Tai Chi Chuan, it has a much broader range of techniques, suitable in a wider range of situations. This has made it adaptable to a wide range of body physiques, personalities, and lifestyles. Hapkido is currently practiced by a diverse range of men, women, and children of all ages; working professionals; gifted athletes; the physically impaired; those simply seeking physical exercise; as well as military and law enforcement professionals.

Hapkido began in Korea and grew into an international style. Many of its early pioneers now reside and teach in the United States. The art is currently practiced in more than 100 countries and continues to expand rapidly worldwide.

Other Eclectic Arts

Hapkido evolved during the middle of the twentieth century by selectively fusing a wide range of existing martial skills with new innovations. The sources for much of Hapkido's technical material also served as the foundation for other twentieth century martial arts such as Taekwondo, Judo, Aikido, and modern Jujutsu. As a result, many similarities in technique are noticeable, although all of these arts tend to be more specifically focused on particular technique areas. Taekwondo emphasizes strikes and kicks, and is rapidly evolving into a major international sport. Judo is primarily a sport based on throwing and ground holds. Aikido focuses on nonviolent blending with submission joint locks, holds, and takedowns. Jujutsu emphasizes joint locks, holds, throws, and sometimes a limited number of strikes.

Other eclectic martial arts which blend a range of different techniques are listed in the chart at right. Some of these systems are fairly obscure or limited to specific geographic areas. Of these arts, Tai Chi Chuan probably possesses the largest number of practitioners, but is rarely practiced in its entirety. Kuk Sool Won and Hwa Rang Do, two Korean martial arts, are also fairly well established in specific regions. Further information on Hapkido and its relationship to the martial arts as a whole can be found in the author's 1136-page book.

Comparison of Eclectic Arts

Martial Art	Origin	Date	Characteristics
Hapkido	Korea	20 c.	Combines all major technique areas: strikes, holds, throws, weapons, internal arts, and healing.
Aiki-Jujutsu	Japan	12 c.	Combines joint locks, holds, throws, and a limited number of strikes.
Aikido	Japan	20 c.	Non-violent joint locks, holds, and takedowns; occasional strikes; evolved from Aki-Jujutsu.
Bando	Burma	15 c.	Combines strikes and grappling. Stresses initial retreat and attacks from outside attacker's arms.
Cha-yon Ryu	USA	20 c.	Combines Hapkido, Taekwondo, Shaolin Kung Fu, and Shito Ryu Karate.
Cuong Nhu	Vietnam	1965	Shotokan Karate blended with Aikido, Judo, Wing Chun, Vovinam, Tai Chi, and boxing.
Hanmudo	Korea/USA	1989	Outgrowth of Hapkido, Kuk Sool Won and other Korean arts; comprehensive eclectic system.
Han Pul	Korea	1963	Outgrowth of Hapkido.
Hwa Rang Do	Korea	20 c.	Evolved from native Korean arts. Combines strikes, holds, throws, weapons, healing, internal arts.
Judo	Japan	19 c.	Primarily a sport involving throws and ground holds; limited strikes; evolved from Jujutsu.
Jujutsu	Japan	17 c.	Combines joint locks, holds, throws, and sometimes a limited number of strikes.
Kajukenbo	Hawaii	1947	Combines Karate, Judo, Jujutsu, Kenpo, and Chinese Boxing; created by 5 individuals.
Kuk Sool Won	Korea	20 c.	System of traditional Korean martial skills: strikes, holds, throws, weapons, healing, internal arts.
Lua	Hawaii	18 c.	Possibly extinct. Combined strikes and grappling; relied heavily on knowledge of anatomy.
Mu-Tau Pankration	Greece/USA	20 c.	Greek Pankration fused with Thai kick boxing and Savate; combines strikes and grappling.
Nippon Kenpo	Japan	20 c.	Combines Judo, Karate, and Aikido techniques.
Sambo	Russia	20 c.	Russian folk wrestling styles fused with elements of Judo, Jujutsu, and Freestyle Wrestling.
Shintaido	Japan	1966	Combines Karate, Judo, Jujutsu, Kendo, Bojutsu, and Shiatsu; uses soft circular motions.
Shooto (Shoot Wrestling)	Japan	20 c.	Sport blending Sambo, Judo, Jujutsu, Wrestling, and Thai Boxing; combines strikes and grappling.
Silat	Malay Peninsula	14 c.	Native arts of Indonesia, Malaysia, and Philippines. Blends strikes, grappling, weapons and dance.
Taekwondo	Korea	20 c.	Karate-like style emphasizing kicks; limited use of joint lock holds.
Tai Chi Chuan	China	14 c.	Combines strikes, holds, throws, weapons and internal arts; in USA primarily practiced for health.

Martial arts, like people, are imbued at the moment of their birth with an essential structure which will define the remainder of their existence. In a person, this is called one's "true nature." It is that fundamental set of qualities that makes something wholly unique unto itself, like no other. Understanding our true nature is essential, since it helps us determine the course of events which allow us to grow and prosper. For martial artists, understanding the roots of their style is vital, since the roots define the art, determining the

HISTORY

manner by which the art will grow and evolve over time. For novices, a sense of history gives them a connection to the past and to a tradition greater than themselves, while for masters, a sense of history is crucial if they wish to be a vital part of a living, evolving martial art, such as Hapkido. A collective understanding of Hapkido's origins, philosophy, and techniques thus allows us to build on its foundation in a way that permits infinite diversity of expression, while retaining those essential qualities that make it only Hapkido.

The Evolution of Martial Arts

The history of the martial arts is essentially an oral tradition. Very little was actually written down until recent times. When one begins examining a broad range of martial arts, it becomes quickly evident that much of their history is contradictory. It is not uncommon to find a particular martial art tracing its roots to the "dawn of time." Specific histories are often touted as fact when they may be little more than anecdotes, or a loose collection of unsubstantiated myths.

The history of most martial arts are intimately entwined with those of the civilizations and cultures with which they are associated. Some ancient cultures left written or visual evidence, others did not.

Fighting skills have of course existed since the dawn of time and developed concurrently in many different geographic regions. These early skills, used by primitive humans for hunting and self-protection, eventually evolved into more sophisticated martial arts. As the modes of travel and communication evolved, cross-cultural influences and wars allowed neighboring societies to observe and absorb martial skills from outside sources. Buddhism, an important element in Korean, Chinese, and Japanese cultures, is known to have originated in India and subsequently spread throughout Central, East, and Southeast Asia. Many Buddhist and Taoist monks practiced martial arts and transmitted their ideas and techniques across cultures.

The earliest written evidence of specific empty-hand arts appears in Egypt, Greece, Crete, and India, although it is likely indigenous martial systems existed in other areas as well. It is thought that the migration of martial arts from China and India to neighboring regions influenced the development of native arts throughout Asia. Among the arts emerging between 400 and 1650 are: Aiki-Jujutsu, Bushido, Capoeri, Chin Na, Chinese Boxing, Jojutsu, Kenjutsu, Kung Fu, Nen Ryu, Ninjutsu, Silat, Subak, Sumo, Tai Chi Chuan, Te, Yawara, and Win Chun.

Hapkido's Roots

Hapkido evolved during the middle of the twentieth century by selectively fusing a wide range of existing martial skills, with new innovations. The basis for much of Hapkido's technical material is thought to come from Daito Ryu Aiki-Jujutsu, a Japanese art, which was reinterpreted and integrated with a broad range of native Korean philosophical ideas and martial techniques. Consequently, to understand Hapkido's roots, one must trace the evolution of both Japanese and Korean martial arts. Such an exercise also reveals Hapkido's relationship to other twentieth century arts such as Aikido, Judo, Jujutsu, Taekwondo, and Korean eclectic styles such as Kuk Sool Won and Hwa Rang Do.

Early Korean Arts

The Korean peninsula was first inhabited around 30,000 BC, when nomadic tribes from Central and Northern Asia migrated into the area. The earliest outside influences absorbed by these tribes likely came through contact with the Chinese, who established commanderies (outposts) in the northern part of the Korean peninsula, from around 108 BC. Constant wars with the Chinese forced these scattered tribal settlements to gradually coalesce into larger political entities, eventually leading to the formation of three powerful kingdoms: Koguryŏ, Silla, and Paekche. This marked the beginning of the Three Kingdoms Period (18 BC – AD 668).

During this period, Korean arts, architecture, literature, politics, and military arts flourished, as Chinese influences continued to be assimilated and reinterpreted in a uniquely Korean manner. Buddhism gradually became the state religion of all three kingdoms, and was eventually transmitted to Japan by way of Paekche. Increasing contact between the cultures of Korea, Japan, and China not only influenced their societies, but their native martial arts as well.

Wall painting depicting empty-hand fighting. Ceiling of Muyong-Chong tomb, AD 3 – AD 427, Three Kingdoms Period.

Native Korean martial arts are thought to have first emerged sometime during the Three Kingdoms Period (18 BC – AD 668). During this time, Korean martial arts did not possess a single umbrella-name. Instead, it is believed that specific skills were grouped into technique areas, which were labeled using generic terms. Some of these terms are:

Su Bak	(punching and butting)
T'ae Kyŏn	(kicking)
Kag Ju	(throwing)
Kung Sa	(archery)
Ki Ma Sa Bŏp	(horse archery)
Tan Gŏm Sul	(short-knife)
Kŏm Sul Bŏp	(sword skills)
Su Yŏng Bŏp	(fighting in water)

Note that these are not the names of specific martial arts styles or systems, although they are often used incorrectly in this context. While it has been recorded that martial arts training was taken seriously and contests were popular, there are unfortunately no surviving written accounts describing these native martial systems or their specific techniques. The limited information we do have comes mostly from paintings, artifacts, and two ancient Korean manuscripts: the *Samkuk Saki* ("Three Kingdoms History"), written in the twelfth century, and the *Samkuk Yusa* ("Three Kingdoms Memorabilia"), written in the thirteenth century. Ancient Chinese and Japanese texts also make occasional reference to Korean martial arts.

It was during the Three Kingdoms Period that two notable warrior classes evolved: the *Sun Bi* ("intelligent-brave"), and later, the *Hwa Rang* ("flower of youth"). The Hwa Rang emerged in the Silla kingdom about 550. In addition to being warriors, they are reputed to have established a high moral code of conduct and were schooled in the intellectual and cultural arts of the time. They were later instrumental in unifying Korea and are also thought to have influenced development of Japanese Bushido ("way of the warrior"), a code of ethics followed by the Japanese warrior-classes. This early transmission of

Korean martial arts may have occurred during the Three Kingdoms Period, when Korean culture was first exported to Japan. For example, architects from Korean Paekche were heavily involved in the proliferation of temple building which occurred in Japan during the sixth century. In fact, there were times during Japan's early history when there were more Koreans involved in secular and religious positions than Japanese.

The Korean peninsula was first unified in 668 when the Silla kingdom conquered Koguryŏ and Paekche. This unification would last through various changes in governments until the mid-twentieth century. For the next 800 years, Korean martial arts went through various periods of advance and decline, depending upon the prevailing political climate and the needs of the people. Around 1100, the generic term *Yu Sul* (meaning "soft arts" or "soft method") emerged as an umbrella term for a range of soft-style martial techniques. Yu Sul is said to have been characterized by throws (mechigi), grappling (kuchigi), and attacks to vital points (kuepso chirigi). Kuepso Chirigi is the Korean equivalent of Japanese Atemi and Chinese Tien Hsueh and Dim Mok—all of which were integrated into many contemporary arts.

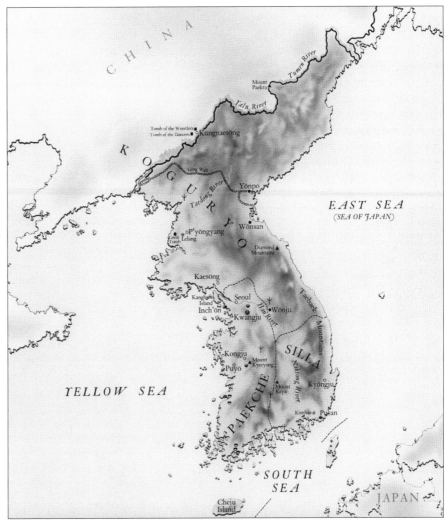

Korean peninsula during Three Kingdoms Period (18 BC – AD 668). Maps courtesy of the Victoria and Albert Museum.

Sometime after 1400 more sophisticated empty-hand fighting systems evolved. Kwon Bŏp emerged as an umbrella term for Korean empty-hand techniques. Ssirüm was a system of grappling skills, with roots in Mongolian wrestling forms. Pakchigi was a system of head-butting, popular in northern Korea. Kag Sul and T'ae Kyŏn were systems emphasizing kicks, and Su Sul was a system of empty-hand techniques derived from sword skills. At some point, Kag Sul eventually came to be called T'ae Kyŏn, and Su Sul to be called Subyukta (art of hand techniques). Subyukta has also been referred to as Su Bak, Su Bak Ki, and Su Bak Do. T'ae Kyŏn was widely practiced and continued to evolve into the twentieth century.

Many of the philosophical ideas and martial techniques found throughout these systems, would eventually be integrated into Hapkido and other modern Korean martial arts.

Early Japanese Arts
Native Japanese martial arts, now called Yawara (ancient Jujutsu), are thought to have first emerged sometime before 500. These fighting skills are believed to be the ancient precursor of Aiki-Jujutsu and later Jujutsu systems. Whether these arts were infused with seizing techniques from Korea or China is not certain. Some contemporary historians believe that the technical basis for Daito-Ryu Aiki-Jujutsu was originally transmitted from Korean Paekche to Japan, by Korean monks during the sixth century. If this is true, these arts were probably assimilated and reinterpreted to suit the needs of Japanese culture.

According to legend, around 850 Prince Teijun, son of Japanese Emperor Fujiwara Seiwa, developed a system of martial techniques (now called Aki-Jujutsu), that were secretly passed down through his progeny. The system was eventually inherited by Shinra Saburo Minimoto Yoshimitsu (1045–1127), who is said to have established the Daito Ryu system of Aiki-Jujutsu. According to legend, Yoshimitsu developed joint lock techniques by dissecting the bodies of convicts.

Daito Ryu continued to be passed down through the centuries, eventually inherited by Tanomo Saigo (1830–1903), who passed it on to Sokaku Takeda (1859–1943). By this time the art was characterized as a comprehensive martial system comprising joint locks, throws chokes, and some strikes. Takeda described Aki-Jujutsu in a 1930 newspaper interview:

"This technique is a perfect self-defense art where you avoid being cut, hit or kicked, while at the same time you don't hit, kick or cut. As the attack comes you handle it expediently using the power of your opponent. So even women and children can execute these techniques." (Tokyo Asahi, 1930)

Korean Chronology

Scholars and historians generally define Korean history according to the following time periods.

Neolithic	c. 4000 – 1000 BC
Bronze Age	c. 900 – 400 BC
Iron Age	400 – 200 BC

Division between North and South

Chinese Commanderies	108 BC – AD 313
Three Han States	0 – AD 200
Mahan	
Chinhan	
Pyŏnhan	

Three Kingdoms

Koguryŏ	37 BC – AD 668
Paekche	18 BC – AD 663
Early Silla	57 BC – AD 668

United Silla	668 – 935
Koryŏ	935 – 1392
Chosŏn (Yi Dynasty)	1392 – 1910
Japanese Colonial Period	1910 – 1945

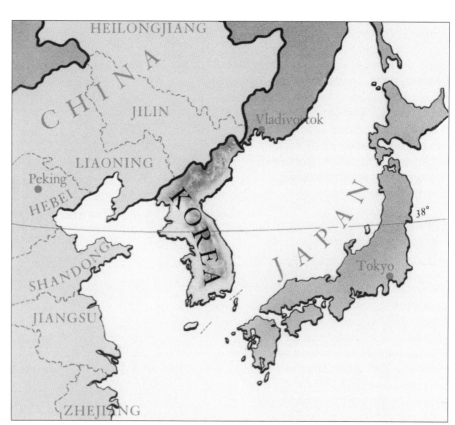

Korea and neighboring regions before 1945. After 1945 Korea was partitioned into North Korea and South Korea.

The Birth of Hapkido

From the 1890s to 1945, Korea was involved in frequent conflicts with and between China and Japan. During this period, many Koreans learned extensively about martial arts being practiced in these countries. As a result, many foreign skills were fused into native Korean martial arts. Tang Soo Do, Kong Soo Do, Su Bak Ki, and Tae Soo Do were some of the twentieth century hard-style martial arts that resulted and later evolved into Taekwondo.

In 1910, the Japanese annexed Korea, abolished the Korean monarchy and outlawed all Korean martial arts. During this time many Koreans studied Japanese Jujutsu, Judo, and Kendo while continuing to practice native martial arts in secret. It is thought that Korean monasteries may have played an important role in preserving many of the native arts.

In the following decades, in the face of continued public unrest and intermittent guerrilla activity, Japanese rule became progressively more brutal. Censorship tightened, the teaching of Korean history and culture was banned, the Japanese language was made mandatory instruction in all schools, and all public signs were required to be in Japanese. As World War II approached, hundreds of thousands of Korean laborers were drafted to assist the Japanese Army in Korea and China—essentially slave labor. Most Koreans view this 36-year period as one of attempted cultural genocide, in which an entire generation lost its freedom and cultural identity. Even today the scars are evident.

Yong-Sul Choi (1904–1986), a pivotal Hapkido pioneer, was taken to Japan around 1912, probably as a child-laborer. Choi is believed to have studied Daito Ryu Aiki-Jujutsu under Grandmaster Sokaku Takeda during the next 30 years, until Takeda's death in 1943. Daito Ryu records do not record Choi's training, although this is not surprising since he was non-Japanese, and discrimination against Koreans was common at this time. It is believed that Choi lived in Takeda's household, either as an adopted member of

Takeda's family (unlikely), or a servant (more likely). During this period, the Japanese forced emigrant Koreans to change their names to Japanese names. "Asao Yoshida" is believed to be the name Takeda gave Choi. Choi's specific role in Daito Ryu Aki-Jujutsu has been widely disputed. In oral history, he has been characterized as everything from a manservant present at training sessions, to one of Takeda's chief instructors.

In attempting to understand Choi's relationship to Takeda, one must understand the social order of the times. Takeda was the last in a long line of prestigious Japanese Samurai. The Japanese considered themselves a "divine race." During this period, Koreans existed on the lowest rung of the Japanese social order, and were commonly used as servants or laborers. This idea of racial superiority was so deeply ingrained in Japanese society, it would have been socially unacceptable for Takeda to acknowledge Choi as anything other than a servant, regardless of how much he liked him. Regardless of Choi's specific role in Japan, there is little doubt that he returned to Korea with formidable martial arts skills.

Korea after 1945

In 1945, World War II ended and Korea regained its independence from Japan. The post-war period was an extremely fertile time for Korean martial arts, as many traditional styles were being rediscovered and synthesized into new eclectic styles. Many arts which had been practiced in secret for decades were being taught publicly for the first time, as various masters vied for public recognition. In decades to come, younger Korean martial artists would also attempt to rediscover and reorganize traditional martial skills into new comprehensive systems that would preserve their national character and prevent them from becoming extinct.

Sometime around 1945 Yong-Sul Choi returned to Korea and began teaching an art he called *Yu Sul* (no relation to ancient Korean Yu Sul). It is thought that Choi initially taught a

pure form of Daito Ryu Aiki-Jujutsu, but adopted the generic Korean term *Yu Sul* ("soft arts") to make the art more palatable to Koreans, who reacted negatively to anything Japanese. At some point, Choi changed the name to *Yu Kwon Sul* ("soft fist arts"), to distinguish it from Judo ("Yudo" in Korean), which possessed the same meaning as Yu Sul. Whether Choi fused Daito-Ryu Aki-Jujutsu with the reemerging native Korean styles he was encountering is unknown. Many believe he continued to teach and practice unmodified Daito-Ryu Aiki-Jujutsu throughout his life.

Choi's most prominent early students were Bok-Sub Suh (1948–1959), Han-Jae Ji (1949–1956) and Moo-Hong Kim (1953–1959). According to Ji and Suh, Choi also referred to the art he studied in Japan as *Yawara.* During the late 1950s and through the 1960s, some of Choi's top students further developed their own ideas independently. Some established new martial arts; others—most notably Han-Jae Ji and Moo-Hong Kim—contributed many innovations (particularly kicks), greatly expanding Hapkido's foundation.

Until the 1960s Hapkido went by various names, including *Yu Sul, Yu Kwon Sul, Hapki Yu Kwon Sul, Kido,* and *Hapkido.* It is possible that techniques from related arts such as Bi Sul, Ho Shin Do, and Yudo (Judo) were also absorbed into Hapkido. Interviews with many martial artists active at that time suggest that there was substantial contact between these various eclectic styles, as practitioners studied with different masters to enrich their training.

By 1965 the name Hapkido was commonly in use and the style was considered a major Korean art, with government recognition. Eventually, many Hapkido masters emigrated overseas and established the art globally, particularly in North America. Today the number of Hapkido practitioners in the United States ranks second only to Korea. A more detailed history, with historical photos, charts, early logos, and martial genealogies, can be found in the author's 1136-page Hapkido book.

A martial art's philosophical system defines the moral and spiritual values embraced by its practitioners, and determines the manner in which the art is practiced, including technique preferences. The technical differences between most martial arts are defined by the unique ways in which they use and combine martial skills. This is largely determined by matters of philosophy, as the techniques themselves are often very similar. Hapkido philosophy is an outgrowth of East Asian philosophy, which has historically been defined by

PHILOSOPHY

Buddhism, Taoism, and Confucianism. Many East Asian martial arts share similar roots, and therefore, distinct philosophical similarities. The following pages briefly outline the fundamental concepts embraced by virtually all Hapkido systems. It is not necessary for one to have a background in Asian philosophy to understand these concepts; however, it will lead to a deeper understanding of the inherent relationship between all martial arts. A detailed chapter on Asian philosophy can be found in the author's 1136-page book.

Hapkido's Purpose

Hapkido's essential purpose is expressed in the meanings attributed to its name. *Hapkido* is a Korean word coined from three separate word-concepts: Hap, Ki, and Do. In the Korean language, *Hap* is the root form for words which mean "harmony," "coming together," or "coordinating." *Ki* means "universal life force" or "energy." *Do* means "the way," "method," or "path." Thus, the name Hapkido was felt to symbolize the idea of "becoming at one with the universe" or "harmonizing mind, body, and spirit with nature." On a more literal level it can also be interpreted as "the way of harmonious power" or "the method of harmonizing energy."

Fundamental Beliefs

A fundamental belief of Hapkido is the idea that martial arts training is primarily a means to physical health, mental well-being, spiritual growth, and perfection of character. This occurs through contemplation and rigorous physical training, which prepares the mind and body for the ongoing difficulties and challenges of life. Supreme confidence in one's ability to transcend violence leads to a peaceful and benevolent nature. The acquisition of fighting skills is considered to be of secondary importance and is often thought of as the *physical* means to a *spiritual* end. Combative techniques are used only for self-defense or the protection of others. Of course, people practice Hapkido for many other reasons as well, such as increasing health, fitness, confidence, and mental and emotional stability. Nonetheless, the integration of martial arts training into all aspects of one's daily life is considered to be an important fundamental objective in all Hapkido training.

Moral Values

Hapkido's moral values are similar to the values stressed throughout society as a whole. They are meant to promote a healthy individual in a healthy society, and evolved from various philosophical and religious traditions. Specific written listings usually

Harmony of body, mind, and spirit within one's environment is a fundamental long-term objective of Hapkido training.

vary between individual schools. Generally, they encompass the following concepts:

- Respect for life
- Respect for society
- Respect for oneself
- Honoring commitments
- Helpfulness to others
- Kindness
- Tolerance
- Patience
- Loyalty
- Courage
- Integrity
- Perseverance
- Honesty
- Modesty
- Compassion
- Appropriate use of force

Although Hapkido's moral values are an outgrowth of Asian religious traditions, the study of Hapkido is non-denominational. Students are not required to change their religious beliefs. A Hapkidoist's personal system of moral values can come from any of the world's great religions or wisdom

traditions; or it can be the result of a secular inwardly directed spiritual process, such as meditation or thoughtful introspection. Regardless of the source, the process of ingraining basic moral values into one's being is an essential aspect of all martial arts training. Sparring is one of the arenas in which our spiritual strengths and weaknesses are frequently magnified (e.g., anger, jealousy, egotism, the need to subjugate others, etc.). In this respect, sparring not only refines physical skills but purifies spiritual and emotional values as well.

Aesthetics

Hapkido does not possess any particular aesthetic concepts that govern the execution of technique, as do Bersilat, Capoeira, Wu Shu, or other martial arts in which visual form or dance are important elements. Hapkido does have a distinct visual style, often described as fast, fluid, circular, spinning, and sometimes acrobatic. However, these visual qualities are entirely a result of practical considerations, not aesthetics. Hapkido's unique qualities are often emphasized during public demonstrations or formal promotions.

PHILOSOPHICAL PRINCIPLES

All martial arts are defined by specific philosophical ideas that determine the manner in which the art is practiced. Hapkido is defined by three fundamental concepts:

• Harmony Theory
• Water Theory
• Circle Theory

These concepts, which evolved from Asian philosophy as a whole, have both a physical and a spiritual component to them. Their "spiritual" side influences one's actions in life, whereas their "physical" side influences how physical techniques are executed.

Harmony Theory (Hwa)

The harmonizing of body, mind, and spirit within one's environment is a fundamental long-term goal of Hapkido training. When all these elements act in harmony, technique becomes fluid, continuous, and instinctive. Every action becomes purposeful, perfectly linked to the moment of its existence. The martial artist no longer responds in the mundane sense (think, then react)—thought and action merge into a single, purposeful act. This state of harmony is not just for fighting, but should pervade all aspects of one's life. If you are truly in harmony with yourself and the world, it is likely you may never need to fight, physically or otherwise. This concept is fundamental to Taoist thought, which asserts that when life takes its natural course, harmony with nature and the correct flow of existence are assured. Closely related to Harmony Theory are the concepts of *empty mind* and *total awareness*. Products of a harmonized mind, they are defined as follows.

Empty Mind

Empty mind, or mind-of-no-mind, is a concept involving mental preparation, which is an outgrowth of Zen Buddhism (called Sŏn Buddhism in Korea). It is characterized as centering, emptying, or quieting the mind, and is often an objective of meditation. This centering of the mind heightens awareness and relaxes musculature, thereby decreasing physical response time. In combat or other highly stressful situations, a relaxed mind free of emotion is better able to concentrate on matters at hand. You move, think, and respond more quickly, and begin to operate on an intuitive level. This relaxed state of focused concentration defines any great athlete in action. It is often described as "being in the moment" or "playing in the zone."

Total Awareness

Total awareness is an altered state of mind based on experience and instinct. It is characterized by calmness of mind, intuitive response, and detachment from life-and-death concerns. In Western thought it is related to the idea of a sixth sense, to which one responds with an uncanny sense of purpose, suggesting a paranormal awareness or precognition of events. This altered state of mind can also be used to expand or compress one's perceptions of time, so that events are perceived outside the framework of ordinary consciousness. A common example is the perception of events one experiences during an automobile accident, where one second seems to take thirty seconds, allowing one to react in ways which may save one's life. Theoretically, developing mind-power skills allows one to control these functions at will and apply them to self-defense.

Water Theory (Yu)

Water Theory relates one's actions in life to the qualities of *flowing water*. The ancients observed that water was a powerful force in nature: Water always found the flaw in a vessel and could penetrate the smallest hole. Water flowing in a river always exerted constant pressure, eventually overwhelming whatever stood in its path. Over time a single persistent drip could wear a hole through stone. A winding stream always found its way around the obstacles placed in its path.

As defined by water theory, constant pressure, penetration, persistence, adaptability, constant flow, and softness are the key qualities that characterize a Hapkidoist's combative tactics and basic approach to life.

Constant pressure refers to constantly striving toward your goals. In terms of self-defense, this means putting constant physical and psychological pressure on your opponents, never allowing them to recover once you have the advantage. *Penetration* means breaking down or passing through obstacles that prevent you from attaining your goals, seizing the smallest opportunity. *Persistence* means constantly directing your resources against an obstacle until it crumbles, never giving up, no matter how long it takes. *Adaptability* means adjusting positively to the changing circumstances of life, and finding the optimum path, while always maintaining your true nature. *Constant flow* means maintaining a continuous flow of energy as you engage an obstacle. *Softness* means cultivating the loving, gentle way; and blending with the greater flows of energy you might encounter.

Circle Theory (Wŏn)

The circle is a universal symbol found in many cultures. Rich in meanings, it has come to symbolize a variety of concepts including: totality, wholeness, perfect unity, recurrence, self-containment, infinity, eternity, time enclosing space, and timelessness.

Hapkido's ranking system, and that of many martial arts, is cyclical in nature. The student begins as a white belt and progresses through the colored ranks until one is a 10th degree black belt, at which time the Grandmaster again wears a white belt, symbolic of the return to the beginning and the start of a new cycle of learning.

The circle has great relevance in Hapkido's martial techniques as well. Ancient martial artists believed that circular techniques and movements were effective because they harmonized one with one's opponent, one's self, and the universe. If one was not at harmony when fighting, the chances of defeat were much greater since one would not only be battling an opponent, but also one's self and the universe. The technical aspect of Circle Theory is discussed on the following page under *Circular Movement*.

TECHNICAL PRINCIPLES

Today there are a many different styles of Hapkido being practiced. Nonetheless, one finds certain core technical principles that are common to all. While these principles may be expressed differently in different styles, they generally involve the following key concepts:

- Redirection of Force
- Blending with Force
- Constant Movement, Varied Rhythm
- Circular Movement
- Ki-Power
- Live-Hand

Redirection of Force

In Hapkido, an attack is rarely met head-on. Power against power, which is often preferred in "hard-styles," is generally discouraged, since the risk of breaking your bones or damaging your body is significant, particularly against more powerful opponents. From the standpoint of physics it is also a highly inefficient use of energy. It takes far more force to directly stop or push back an attack than it does to deflect or absorb it.

In Hapkido, an opponent's power is used against that person whenever possible. By manipulating the opponent's balance or redirecting the person's external force and internal energy (Ki) you increase the efficiency of your own techniques. Redirection of force is particularly important when facing multiple attackers. By redirecting their movements it may be possible to use them as shields or cause collisions in which one opponent is hurled into the other. Such "redirection of an attacker's force against other attackers' forces" is a highly efficient use of your own energy—a hallmark of Hapkido.

Generally speaking, the force directing an opponent's attack—for instance a punch, kick or charge—can be redirected in one of four possible ways: opposing, deflecting, absorbing, and joining. Some of these methods are more desirable than others, but all are effective given the right situation. This is expanded upon in the author's 1136-page Hapkido book.

Blending with Force

In Hapkido the defender attempts to blend or unite with the attacker's force. This can be thought of metaphorically, as occupying the calm space within a tornado, or joining with the force of the tornado by matching its speed and motion. This is accomplished by knowing when to give way and when to attack. Consequently, Hapkido tactics often alternate between highly aggressive and defensive modes, depending upon the needs of a given situation. In practical terms this requires footwork, timing, speed, power, and versatility—the essential qualities of any good fighter. Extreme blending is commonly seen in martial arts such as Tai Chi Chuan and Aikido. Hapkido blending is not usually this extreme.

Constant Movement, Varied Rhythm

Hapkido fighting technique is characterized by a constant, varied flow of striking, blocking, holding, and throwing techniques executed from highly mobile stances. Footwork and body movement is constant and may incorporate circular, spinning, or off-axis movements. By constantly varying body positioning and the rhythm of attack, you become much more difficult to target and are much more likely to disorient and frustrate your opponent. This becomes even more important when dealing with multiple attackers. Varied rhythm is achieved by:

- Varying speed of movement or attack
- Abrupt changes in tactics
- Abrupt changes in technique (strike, throw)
- Varying target height of attack (high, low)
- Switching between offense and defense

Circular motions being used to apply a throw

Circular Movement

Many Hapkido techniques are made up of circular movements. Large or small circles can be seen in the motions of strikes, blocks, holds, joint locks, chokes, throws, footwork, and general body movements. These circular movements can be either large or small, depending upon the technique or the particular system. Some Hapkido systems focus on larger movements. Others stress smaller circles with a more direct application of force. In the hands of skilled masters, many Hapkido techniques are applied using small, tight circular motions—especially joint locks.

Circular motion is also applied by spinning. This can be seen in certain strikes, spin kicks, and throws, in which fast body-spins create devastating speed and power. This a result of physics. For example, the force of a spin kick at impact is mostly dependent upon the foot's velocity, weight, and muscle force. The velocity of the foot is influenced by the length of the leg. The longer the leg, the greater the velocity.

The relationship between force and the length of your leg can be better understood by considering another example. Visualize a record turntable revolving at a constant speed (typically measured in revolutions per minute or "rpm"). A coin is placed 1 inch from the center. A second coin is placed at the outside edge. With each revolution of the platter, the coin on the outside travels a much greater distance than the coin near the center. It does this in the same duration of time; therefore, its velocity is significantly greater.

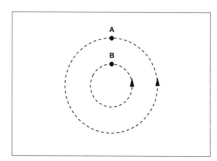
Impact Force: A is greater than B at the same rpm

Ki-Power

The word *Ki* (also written as *Gi*, *Qi*, or *Chi*) is essentially untranslatable, although it is often described as the "vital energy" or "life force" that permeates the universe, flowing through and animating all things. It has been the basis of Oriental medicine for thousands of years.

In Hapkido, the term "Ki-power" refers to the use of *Ki* (internal energy) and *adrenaline* to assist the application of a technique, such as a strike, hold, or escape. Although skillful technique does not require the use of Ki-power to be highly effective, focusing Ki will increase a technique's efficiency (see photo at lower-right). When fighting a highly skilled or overpowering opponent, the addition of Ki-power may be the difference between a technique that works and one that fails. In Hapkido, Ki-power is used as the basis of many movements, and is developed through specific exercises, meditation, and Tanjon Breathing. For serious practitioners attempting to develop their Ki, a variety of factors must be in balance—diet, air quality, emotional state, sleep, sexual activity, and the level of stress in your life all affect the levels of Ki and adrenaline in your body.

Adrenaline

Although no one knows exactly what Ki is (from a scientific point of view), the functions of adrenaline are fairly well understood. *Epinephrine,* commonly called adrenaline, is a hormone produced by the adrenal glands that stimulates the nervous system. The adrenal glands are two small dissimilar shaped glands, one located above each kidney,

consisting of the cortex, which secretes hormones, and the medulla, which secretes adrenaline. When adrenaline is released during normal exercise, or at moments of high stress, it produces cardiac stimulation, constriction or dilation of blood vessels, and bronchial relaxation. Athletes with high levels of adrenaline in their systems have reported elevated performances, characterized by increased speed and power, and heightened emotions. Excessive release of adrenaline into your system is unhealthy, and often the result of an overly stressful lifestyle. In Hapkido's combative applications, there are methods for releasing adrenaline into your system, such as mental visualization, or vibrating the molars by grinding or emitting an energy-harmonizing shout, called *Kihap* in Korean (see later section, *Breathing + Meditation*).

Live-Hand

The term *Live-Hand* refers to specific hand formations which are used to increase the flow of Ki into the hands and arms. This increases arm strength and power when most needed, such as during a wrist escape or application of a joint lock hold. Live-Hand techniques involve visualization, breath control, and tensing of the fingers, hands, and arms. Concentration and focus are very important, as is practice. The use of a Live-Hand is typically characterized by extending one or more fingers and breathing out as a specific technique is applied.

In Hapkido, Live-Hands are an ingredient part of many striking, blocking, holding, and throwing techniques. They are very important

in Tanjon Breathing and in wrist escapes. At one time, Live-Hands were used extensively. In recent years, the use of extended fingers in combat has fallen into disfavor among some practitioners due to their increased vulnerability to attack or damage. Today many stylists restrict Live-Hand use in fighting to wrist escapes, well-controlled breaking blocks, or holds in which the extra power is often needed and the fingers are well-protected from being grabbed or broken.

Typical Live-Hand Formations

The photographs shown below illustrate two typical Live-Hand formations. In the far-left photograph, a basic Live-Hand is formed by spreading all five fingers very wide, with the thumb slightly bent. This hand formation expands and hardens the wrist and forearm, concentrating Ki in the hand and fingertips. It is often used to apply wrist escapes, blocks, and arm bars. In the middle photo, a Live-Hand is formed by closing the hand, with only the forefinger and thumb extended (in some techniques, the thumb may be tucked). This formation is usually used when gripping an object, such as an attacker's limb or your own weapon; it is also used in a traditional Hammer Fist strike, in which you hit with the bottom of the fist.

Further Study

Hapkido philosophy and Asian philosophy as a whole are discussed in greater detail in the author's comprehensive 1136-page book, *Hapkido: Traditions, Philosophy, Technique.* This larger work also contains a subsection on the unique concepts of Sin Moo Hapkido.

Live-Hand with five fingers spread   Live-Hand with forefinger and thumb extended

Using Live-Hands and Ki-power to escape wrist holds

All techniques observed within the martial arts world can be organized into seven basic categories: striking, avoiding and blocking, holding, throwing, weapons, internal techniques (meditation, breathing, internal energy development), and healing. The differences in technique between most martial arts are defined by the unique manner in which they use or combine one or more of these seven technical categories. Most martial arts place an emphasis on two or three technical areas. Hapkido is somewhat distinct in that it integrates

TECHNIQUE OVERVIEW

all seven areas. The first six areas are emphasized equally during formal training. The seventh area, healing techniques, is usually part of master-level training and focuses on the study of specific healing arts such as acupuncture, massage, herbology, and general medicine. The following pages provide a brief technical overview of Hapkido in its entirety. This is how the art is commonly structured, and is reflected in the organization of this book. All of these techniques are documented in detail in the author's 1136-page Hapkido book.

HAPKIDO TECHNIQUES

Hapkido techniques integrate all of the major technical areas found in the martial arts: strikes, kicks, avoiding movements, blocks, holds, throws, weapons, internal techniques (meditation, breathing, internal energy development), and healing. In practice, martial skills are not thought of as separate technique areas (e.g., holding or throwing), but are combined into a single unified body of techniques designed to respond to particular forms of attack.

Generally, all confrontations or fights can be fundamentally characterized by the presence or absence of weapons. Hapkido techniques fall into three basic categories, reflecting this fundamental nature of confrontation:

- Empty hands against empty hands
- Empty hands against weapons
- Weapons against weapons

All techniques encompass *offensive* and *defensive* modes, against *single* and *multiple* opponents, from the following positions:

- Reclining (on back, side, or front)
- Sitting (seated, kneeling)
- Standing (moving on feet)
- Airborne (jumping or leaping)

The following outline summarizes Hapkido's major techniques by category. It is not meant to be a complete listing of all techniques or an indication of teaching methodology, but rather to provide a general overview of the physical techniques that define Hapkido.

Currently, there is a great deal of variation with respect to specific techniques taught by specific masters and schools. This diversity is a result of Hapkido's extremely complex and varied repertoire, as well as its globally decentralized structure.

Breathing + Meditation

Various forms of breathing and meditation are used to enhance physical performance, focus the mind, increase concentration, and improve health. The ability to channel and control Ki (internal energy) is an important long-term objective of training. Specific techniques vary from system to system.

Revival + Healing

Basic first aid and revival techniques are learned by all practitioners before attaining black belt level. More sophisticated healing techniques are usually acquired by Hapkido masters through the study of a specific healing art of their choice, such as massage, acupuncture, herbology, kinesiology, or general medicine (Eastern or Western).

Stances

Hapkido stances are an integral part of continuous movement. In fact, many schools do not even teach specific stances, but instead focus on footwork and movement. Nonetheless, there are about 22 basic stances, which are freely modified in practical self-defense to create innumerable variations. In this book, basic stances are divided into three categories:

- Relaxed Stances
- Fighting Stances
- Traditional Stances

Movement

Hapkido movement occurs from any possible position, and is characterized by stepping, sliding, running, walking, jumping, turning, spinning, crawling, dragging, rolling, and tumbling. There are about 71 basic forms of movement divided into three basic categories:

- Standing Movement
- Ground Movement
- Transitional Movement

Targets

Hapkido strikes, blocks, holds, throws, and weapon techniques focus on attacking the body's weak points—about 75 anatomical targets and 384 acupoint targets. Of these 384 acupoints, about 83 are commonly used. By black belt level, Hapkidoists acquire a detailed knowledge of human anatomy that allows them to attack with greater effect, without causing unnecessary injury.

Attack Points

These are the specific parts of your body you will use to execute specific techniques. There are about 60 basic body surfaces used for striking, blocking, holding, and throwing. This often involves specific formations of the hands and feet (e.g., a clenched fist). Attack Points are classified into three categories:

- Hand and Arm Formations
- Leg Formations
- Head and Body

Striking Techniques

Hapkido striking techniques use about 60 basic body surfaces to deliver blows. There are more than 200 basic strikes, with numerous variations. They are classified as:

- Hand Strikes
- Lower Arm Strikes
- Elbow Strikes
- Standing Kicks
- Knee Strikes
- Ground Kicks
- Jump Kicks
- Head Strikes
- Body Strikes

Combination Strikes

Multiple strikes can be executed sequentially or simultaneously (e.g., punch and kick at the same time). There are an infinite number of possible combinations; the author's larger book lists more than 200, classified as:

- Arm Strike Combinations
- Kick Combinations
- Mixed Combinations

Avoiding + Blocking Techniques

Blocking techniques use the hands, arms, legs, and torso against all forms of strikes. There are about seven basic avoiding movements and 96 basic blocks, with numerous variations. They are classified as:

- Avoiding Techniques
- Soft Blocks
- Hard Blocks
- Shielding Blocks
- Blocks Against Kicks
- Kicks Used For Blocking

Holding Techniques

Holding techniques are characterized by grabbing, squeezing, pressing, twisting, bending, leveraging, breaking, or strangulation attacks, which are directed to joints, muscles, tendons, ligaments, bones, nerves, acupoints, and blood vessels. Holds are applied to a wide variety of anatomical targets. There are about 176 basic holds, with innumerable variations. They are classified as:

- Wrist Locks
- Arm Locks
- Shoulder Locks
- Finger Locks
- Leg Locks
- Chokes and Head Locks
- Nerve Holds

Throwing Techniques

All major forms of throwing and takedown techniques are used. There are about 132 basic throwing techniques, with innumerable variations. There are eight basic methods of falling (called breakfalls), which incorporate various body motions such as rolling, tumbling, and aerial flips. Throwing techniques are classified as:

- Breakfalls
- Shoulder Throws
- Hip Throws
- Leg Throws
- Hand Throws
- Sacrifice Throws
- Kick-Counter Throws

Weapons Techniques

Weapons techniques are divided into two areas, which encompass both offensive and defensive techniques. In the first area of study, *unarmed techniques* combine strikes, blocks, holds, and throws for use against armed attackers. In the second area of study, *weapon techniques* are integrated with strikes, blocks, holds, and throws for use against armed or unarmed attackers. There are more than 470 basic weapons techniques, with undetermined possible variations. Weapon systems studied in Hapkido include:

- Knife
- Short-Stick
- Long-Staff
- Cane
- Sword
- Rope
- Common Objects
- Defense Against Handgun

Common Objects used as weapons can involve almost any utilitarian object. Master-level training usually includes study of: mini-stick (typically 1/2 in. diameter by 6 in. length), sand throwing, coin throwing, stone throwing (also includes metal marbles), plate throwing, and needle or dart throwing.

Historically, unarmed defenses against handguns were not part of Hapkido weapons training. In recent decades, this material has been incorporated into many Hapkido systems to keep pace with modern needs.

Technique Categories and Self-Defense

Hapkido consists of more than 1,500 major self-defense techniques, with innumerable variations. Some Hapkido systems claim totals ranging from 3,800 to 10,000 skills, although most of these are variations on similar techniques.

For teaching and promotion purposes, self-defense skills are generally organized into the categories listed below. However, in practical application, basic techniques are combined in an instinctive, intuitive, and highly individualized manner. These categories exist only to facilitate learning. Certain aspects of weapons training are no longer being taught, due to emerging legal issues. Self-defense categories include:

Empty Hands Against Empty Hands
- Defense Against Punch
- Defense Against Kick
- Defense Against Holds
- Defense Against Chokes
- Defense Against Joint Locks
- Defense Against Throws
- Ground Defenses
- Defense Using One or No Arms
- Attacking Techniques
- Defense Against Multiple Opponents
- Protecting Another Person

Weapons Techniques
- Knife Techniques
- Short-Stick Techniques
- Long-Staff Techniques
- Cane Techniques
- Sword Techniques
- Rope Techniques
- Common Objects as Weapons
- Defense Against Handgun

PREPARATION

Training Facilities

Martial arts are practiced in a specially designed facility or gymnasium commonly called a *tojang* (Korean) or *dojo* (Japanese). The practice area is designed to facilitate training while protecting the individuals from injury. There should be no sharp corners or dangerous obstructions such as columns, glass cases, furniture, exposed hardware, or low ceilings and light fixtures. There should be adequate room to maneuver without running into walls or other people.

In Hapkido or other arts using throwing techniques, the floor is covered with reinforced, padded mats that protect the trainee by absorbing and cushioning the body during falls. To avoid foot injuries from tripping, the mats must be placed flat without spaces between them. As tears develop, they must be promptly repaired or replaced. Over time, most mats shift from use, and should be periodically adjusted as required.

Originally mats were constructed from a grass or straw-like material. In Japan they are called *tatami* and were also found throughout traditionally furnished homes. Today mats are constructed out of a variety of sophisticated materials including plastics and foams, with common coverings being canvas or vinyl. Mats are available in interlocking sections or continuous rolls from martial arts or gymnastic supply houses. Many training facilities place mats over special wood floors that flex under impact. Crash-pads are also used if more cushioning is needed. Mirrors, punching bags, stretch bars, and various other devices are also used to assist training.

Uniform and Clothing

The jacket, belt, and pants worn during martial arts training is called a *tobok* (Korean) or *dogi* (Japanese). The jacket and pants are normally white, and the belt is color-coded according to the student's rank. The belt is long enough to wrap twice around the waist and then tie in a square knot with two equal ends hanging loosely, 10 to 15 inches beyond the knot.

Martial arts uniforms are manufactured in a variety of fabric weights. Lighter weights are less restrictive of movement. Heavier weights resist tearing during holds and throws. Many practitioners prefer a medium-weight Judo-like uniform that resists tearing but does not hamper striking and kicking movements. One advantage to wearing a heavy uniform is that it more closely approximates the weight of street clothing found in cooler climates.

Other garments often are worn under uniforms to enhance performance and protect the body. Mid-length or full-length tights are worn to support the muscles, retain heat, and wick sweat away from the body's surface. Many athletes also believe they help reduce muscle strains and pulls. Men should always wear appropriate groin support. Women should wear bras designed specifically for active sports. Leotards also are frequently worn for additional support and comfort.

Uniform Styles

Traditional Hapkido uniforms were white. In some systems, master-level practitioners are distinguished by black piping added to the edges of the jacket and along the length of the pants. Currently, a wide variety of uniforms are being used by different schools. Black pants or jackets are frequently worn to designate rank or for the simple goal of looking good. Traditionally, wearing black pants was not an indicator of rank or a matter of fashion, but signified your ability to take a fall. The pants were not dyed black, rather they became dirty (eventually black) through repeated falling. The darkness of the pants indicated the number of falls you had taken, and by inference, your level of expertise. In traditional schools, when you wear black pants you are signalling to everyone that you are capable of falling—and are ready, willing, and able to do so at any time. Today, black uniforms may be worn to signify rank or expertise, but in most schools, represent nothing other than a fashion choice. Similarly, jackets with a diamond pattern are increasingly being seen in many Hapkido schools and associations.

Rank System

In most Korean, Japanese, and Okinawan martial arts, level of skill (rank) is designated by a colored belt worn around the waist. Before the twentieth century, most belts were colorless. Since students were prohibited from washing their belts, the belt grew progressively darker as a result of sweat, grime, mold, and blood until it eventually resembled a blackish color. When the colored belt system came into use, it was organized so that the belt color became progressively darker as the student advanced in rank.

There are approximately 21 levels of rank in Hapkido, with 11 occurring before the black belt levels. The 11 colored ranks below black belt are called grades ("kŭp" in Korean). The 10 ranks of black are referred to as degrees or "dans." Black belt holders also have titles that denote levels of achievement: 1st, 2nd and 3rd degree black belt holders are called assistant instructors or instructors; 4th to 6th degrees are called masters; 7th and 8th degrees are called master instructors; and 9th and 10th degrees are grandmasters.

Ranks in Hapkido are awarded based on skills and the amount of time spent in training at one's current rank. Promotion from one rank to another usually occurs through formal testing, which assesses a candidate's skills according to specific rank requirements. At the discretion of the instructor, ranks may also be awarded based primarily on training time. This is usually done for individuals who exhibit extreme dedication but possess specific physical limitations which make it impossible for them to do certain techniques.

In most Hapkido associations, a black belt may promote individuals as high as two ranks below their own rank. Traditionally, a fourth degree black belt (master-level) was considered the minimum qualification for teaching the art, although many individuals are trained by lower-ranked degrees in regions where high-ranking masters do not exist. Hapkido's ranking system, from lowest to highest rank, is given in the appendix.

The specific skills required for each rank vary by school and association. Typical standards through 4th degree black are listed in the appendix. Skills testing usually ends at 4th degree, after which promotion is based on years of service and contributions to Hapkido. Ninth degrees are promoted by 10th degrees. Tenth degrees are appointed by a federation or a consensus of 9th degrees. They are not self-appointed, or elected by their students. Historically, 10th degree was reserved for the founder or inheritor of a martial art style.

Etiquette

Etiquette is the code of conduct and procedure by which you conduct yourself in the tojang. These traditional procedures are common to many martial arts and have been passed down through the centuries. Historically, many forms of etiquette arose for reasons of safety as well as respect. For example, the custom of shaking hands with one hand placed under the other, was done to show that you had no intention of drawing a weapon. The hands were plainly visible and signaled your peaceful intentions.

Bowing

Bowing, from either a standing or sitting position, is a sign of gratitude and respect found throughout the martial arts world. Westerners often misinterpret this as an act of submission, or see it as part of some deviant totalitarian ideal. This is incorrect. When you bow, it signifies not only respect for your instructors or superiors, but respect for yourself, the art, and "life" in general. It is a symbol of your profound regard and caring for the rights and lives of others. This reflects a basic attitude found throughout East Asian culture. For example, it is usually considered extremely bad form to embarrass or humiliate someone, even if they deserve it. If this happens, the offender is said to "lose face" and must correct the matter through some form of reparation and expression of humility toward the person offended. This form of behavior is quite foreign to many Westerners, for whom personal expression is sometimes placed before the feelings of others.

Bowing is normally done at the beginning and ending of practice sessions, sparring, and drills. You should also bow from the edge of the mat when entering and leaving, or when addressing an instructor.

Formal Sitting Bow

To perform a sitting bow, sit on both knees with your shins flush against the mat, knees shoulder width apart, hips resting on heels, hands on thighs. Bow by placing both palms on the mat in front of your knees, with the fingertips together and turned slightly inward. Bow from the waist as shown. A variation is sometimes used in which the toes and the balls of the feet are placed against the mat.

Informal Standing Bow

To perform a standing bow, place both heels together with toes angled outward. Place your open hands at your side, fingers together, shoulders back. Bow from the waist. The command to bow in Korean is *Kyŏng-nye*.

Addressing Instructors

An instructor is always addressed as *sir* unless permission has been given to call him

Informal Bow from Standing Position

Formal Bow from Kneeling Position

or her by name. In Korean, there are different forms of "sir," depending upon the rank of the person addressed. An instructor is addressed as *sa-bŏm-nim,* a master as *kwan-jang-nim.* Never interrupt while an instructor is speaking, or another student is asking a question; give your full attention, remaining motionless. When an instructor finishes speaking, it is customary to respond by saying *sir, sa-bom-nim,* or *kwan-jang-nim* to signify your understanding and enthusiasm.

School Etiquette

Every school has its own rules of etiquette. Some are very formal, others are quite relaxed. This is not a reflection of quality, but of choice. To assure that you do not cause any disrespect to your instructors, fellow students, or the school in general, always observe the following guidelines:

- Always address an instructor as "sir"
- Always bow when entering or leaving
- Never wear shoes on the mat
- Never wear unapproved or dirty uniforms
- Never sit or lie down unless directed
- Never spar unless directed
- Keep practicing until told to stop
- Never modify practice unless directed
- Always clean the practice area if asked
- Give instructors your full attention when they are speaking, remaining motionless

The Element of Risk

Martial arts can be a safe, rewarding, and physically beneficial practice. There is no reason to suffer debilitating injuries to enjoy its benefits or acquire its skills. However, you must be comfortable accepting the element of risk associated with the style you practice. Your age, health, conditioning, and athleticism all influence the level of risk. Before training and periodically thereafter, obtain a thorough medical examination. Be aware of limitations or existing physical conditions that may affect training. Advise your instructor, and never do *anything* in which you do not feel comfortable or safe. Remember, you are the best judge of your own limits, and the one who must live with the physical results of your actions.

Overview

Many forms of breathing and meditation are used in martial arts to enhance physical performance, focus the mind, increase concentration, improve health, and cultivate spiritual sensitivity. Generally speaking, these techniques are not unique to Hapkido or any other martial art, but come from the broader religious, philosophical, and medical traditions found throughout the East—particularly Buddhism and Taoism. In Hapkido, one of the primary objectives of meditation and controlled breathing is not only to focus the mind, but also to channel and control the circulation of Ki (energy) throughout the body. Eventually this also allows one to gain control of many body functions not normally controllable by conscious mental processes.

The Tanjon

Tanjon is a Korean term for an Asian concept that refers to three regions of the body: the lower-tanjon, middle-tanjon, and upper-tanjon. The *lower-tanjon* is located about 2 inches below the navel and 2 inches below the skin. The lower-tanjon is said to be the center of all vital energy and the foundation of all human power. It is the point where various forms of Ki are absorbed, stored, and distributed to other regions of the body. It is marked by the CO-6 acupoint (also called "Ki Hae," or "Sea of Ki"). When executing martial techniques, the lower-tanjon is the center of balance and the source of mental and physical power. When executing a power technique, such as breaking a board, the martial artist draws his or her power from this region.

The *middle-tanjon* is located at the solar plexus, and is also a reservoir where Ki is produced and gathered.

The *upper-tanjon* is located on the forehead. When it is properly balanced with Ki, the mind is alert and energized.

The proper balance of Ki between the three tanjon regions enhances Ki-flow throughout the body, leading to a clear mind, elevated physical performances, and overall health.

Ki Development

The process of learning to control one's Ki (internal energy) is a fundamental aspect of Hapkido, and is usually organized into three distinct stages. The first stage involves learning to accumulate Ki in specific areas of the body, typically the lower-tanjon. The second stage involves learning to distribute Ki from the lower-tanjon, to other areas of the body. The third stage involves learning to use Ki in specific martial arts techniques. For example, Ki can be used to make the body heavy or light; harden specific parts of the body, making it resistant to damage; numb specific parts of the body so that pain cannot be felt; or increase physical speed and power beyond normal limits. At highly advanced levels, Ki can be projected out into another person for destructive purposes or drained from them to weaken them. These same abilities can also be used to heal.

Channeling Ki on demand is initiated by mental processes or physical techniques, such as controlling the breath, vibrating the molars, or emitting an "energy-shout" (covered on the next page). Awareness of your Ki and an ability to regulate it for specific purposes is developed through meditation exercises involving specific breathing methods, postures, and physical movements. A good teacher is essential. Training time and progress varies widely by individual.

Meditation

There are many forms of meditation, used for a wide variety of purposes. Meditation can lead a person to greater emotional stability and inner peace, and greatly increases one's ability to focus the mind. This ability to focus concentration is essential in learning to harness Ki and control bodily functions. A brief period of meditation before Hapkido practice will help to focus your mind, greatly aiding the learning of new techniques. Virtually all forms of meditation first begin with a conscious awareness of breath. It is this regulation of the mind and the breath that provides the foundation for further Ki development and training.

Typical Breathing Meditation

Assume any comfortable posture. A few common postures are shown at right, although many others are also used. Try to keep the spine elongated, with a slight natural curvature. Don't straighten it unnaturally or slouch. Clear your mind of emotional disturbances and try to become aware of your breath and the muscles that control it. Breathe slowly and deeply down into the abdomen. Focus on being calm, continuous, and uniform, with an equal inhalation-exhalation cycle. The chest should remain mostly stationary. Inhale and exhale through your nose. There are various methods of timing the inhalation and exhalation cycle. In the beginning, just try to breathe with a natural rhythm. Gradually try to extend the length of your breathing cycle. For example: inhale for 8 seconds, exhale for 8 seconds. You can also add resting periods between each breath: inhale for 8, hold for 4, exhale for 8, rest for 4, repeat the cycle.

If you have trouble concentrating, try counting backward from 100 to 1, as you breathe. If you miss a number, begin again. This basic exercise is often used with beginners to develop the ability to focus their mind.

Visualization During Breathing

When you inhale air, it obviously enters your lungs. However, Ki will go where your mind directs it. Creative visualization is considered to be extremely important, and is the primary method by which Ki is channeled to various parts of the body. Thus, when practicing abdominal breathing exercises, it is very important to visualize the Ki traveling to and filling the lower-tanjon region.

There are many different forms of Ki visualization. One is to visualize your nose moving from your head to the GV-4 acupoint on the lumbar spine (other locations are also used). As you inhale, visualize that air and Ki are entering through the GV-4 acupoint (relocated nose), and into the tanjon. As you exhale, visualize your tanjon expelling bad air and Ki through your GV-4 acupoint (relocated nose).

Tanjon Breathing Exercises

Abdominal breathing exercises are commonly practiced in many Hapkido systems. A typical example is shown below. They are primarily used to accumulate Ki in the lower-tanjon and direct it to specific parts of the body—usually the spine, arms, and hands. These exercises are normally practiced daily. The breath cycle is commonly applied as follows (numerous variations exist): Inhale for 8 seconds, press air down into your abdomen and hold your breath for 2 to 8 seconds, exhale for 8 seconds, repeat the cycle. Specific arm movements are coordinated with the breath cycle. During these exercises, try to sense the flow of internal energy within your body. As you inhale, Ki is collected and concentrated in the abdomen. As your arms move, Ki is channeled from the lower-tanjon, through the spine and arms, to the fingertips. A teacher is essential for learning the forms.

The Kihap-Shout

The distinct shout many martial artists emit when executing techniques is essentially breathing meditation converted to dynamic action. In Korean, this energy harmonizing shout is referred to as a *Kihap*. In the Japanese language it is called a *Kiai*.

The word *Ki* is defined as the universal energy or dynamic force that animates all things. The Korean *Hap* is the root form for words which connote harmonizing, coming together, or coordinating. Thus the concept of *Kihap* literally means to harmonize with the dynamic universal life force. The "Kihap-shout" or "energy-harmonizing shout" is a means, then, of coordinating our actions with the flow of energies and events of which we are part. All individual actions and events merge into a single flow. This is what is meant by "being at one with the universe."

The Dynamic Release of Energy

When you execute a punch, kick, or throw, or block a strike, energy is released—typically as a rush of air from the lungs. This exhalation of air, coordinated with muscular tension in the body and throat, creates the deep, roaring growl of the true Kihap-shout. In Hapkido, the Kihap-shout is often performed with the jaw closed and teeth touching. In this situation, the shout is used to produce a vibration in the molar teeth, which stimulates the release of adrenaline into your system. This produces internal energy, which the mind transports and directs into a focused burst of physical speed and power. The Kihap-shout is an integral part of this process, and a reflection of the dynamic release of internal energy. In some systems, different shouts are used for specific actions or events. Some Hapkidoists remain silent. Further material can be found in the author's 1136-page Hapkido book.

Typical Postures and Breathing Exercise

Half Lotus with tips of thumbs, index fingers, and middle fingers lightly touching

Half Lotus with tips of thumbs lightly touching, left fingers over right fingers

Half Lotus with palms facing each other (sensing Ki between them)

Standing position with feet parallel, legs apart, and knees slightly bent

Tanjon Breathing Exercise (pushing forward)

Overview

It is not uncommon for breathing or heart functions to cease when a person is rendered unconscious. This may result from a choke hold cutting off the air or blood supply, or by striking certain acupoints or vital targets. Restoration of breathing and heart functions is often quite simple for someone with proper medical training. For someone without training, or in the absence of immediate attention, an individual might easily die or suffer permanent brain damage.

In the martial arts, Eastern revival methods are often used to revive a person who is dazed or unconscious. Many of these methods evolved during prior centuries, and were secretly studied along with pressure point strikes. During the twentieth century, many of these secret methods gradually became known to the general public.

Today, numerous revival methods exist. This chapter will present those most typically used. These procedures should be learned from a qualified practitioner. They are considered to be "first aid," and are not a substitute for qualified medical attention. In any medical emergency, always seek the aid of qualified medical personnel. Never attempt to move anyone if you suspect serious injuries; you may do more harm than good, and be legally liable.

Legal Concerns

Use of accepted Eastern revival techniques in the United States, which are well established and proven in Asia, may leave you vulnerable to a lawsuit, since they are not currently approved by the American Medical Association. Cardiopulmonary Resuscitation (CPR) and other Western first aid procedures are easily learned and often taught for free at the community level. Incorrect application of Eastern or Western revival techniques may leave you legally responsible for your actions. The material presented in this section is neither an endorsement of, nor a guarantee that any of these techniques will be safe or effective in any medical emergency.

Revival Techniques

The following revival techniques are those most commonly used, and are easily learned. Many others exist, including some that rely on precise pressure point knowledge and Ki manipulation. Before applying any revival technique, check the patient's air passage to make sure it is clear. Food, water, a foreign object, or the tongue can cause a blockage, which must be addressed. Loss of consciousness may be accompanied by cyanosis (bluish or purplish discoloration of skin due to lack of oxygen) or incontinence (inability to control waste functions). Do not attempt to move anyone if you suspect serious injuries (e.g., spinal fracture).

1. Knee-to-Spine Revival

This is used to restore breathing functions or revive a person who has fainted. Maneuver the patient into a sitting position with one leg crossed. Support the head and avoid sharp movements, or you may cause whiplash. Stand behind the patient with your knee pressing into the spine, between the shoulder blades. Spread your fingers and place your hands on the lower chest. Pull back the chest and shoulders as you press your knee forward into the spine. This action draws air into the lungs. When the ribs are open as far as they will go, release them, returning to the starting position. This action expels air from the lungs. This inhalation-exhalation process should be repeated slowly and regularly at a rate of 4 to 6 seconds per cycle (10 to 15 times per minute), until the patient begins breathing without assistance. Your movements should encourage the natural breathing process by opening and closing the diaphragm.

2. Spine-Slap Revival

This is used to restore breathing or revive a person who has fainted. Maneuver the patient into a sitting position, with the legs extended and the hands hanging at the side. Support the head and avoid sharp movements, to avoid whiplash. Kneel to one side of the patient. Support the upper body with your left arm. Form a Palm Hand, placing your middle finger on or near the protruding bone at the base of the neck. Using the lower portion of your palm, hit firmly into the 6th and 7th thoracic vertebras, between the shoulders. This provides a shock that will often initiate breathing. Do not hit so hard as to damage vertebrae or cause whiplash. This is a very old technique, but one that works well.

3. Acupoint Revival

When hitting nerves or acupoints, you may cause someone to faint. If a person is already nervous, fatigued, weak, or hungry, they will be more susceptible. To revive a person who has fainted, press hard with your fingernail at: GV-26 on the upper lip (see 3.1); LI-4 at the back of the hand, in the web of the thumb (see 3.2); or KI-1 on the sole of the foot (see 3.3). Many other acupoint manipulations are used to treat injuries to specific areas of the body. Most require proper medical training.

4. Testicle Revival (lifting and dropping)

This procedure is used to treat a patient whose testicles have been kicked up into his pelvis. It is not used to restore breathing. Place the patient in a sitting position and stand behind him. Wrap your arms under the armpits and clasp your hands together (see 4A). Lift him upward a few inches and let him drop (see 4B–4C), repeating as necessary (usually 6 to 7 times). This jarring motion may cause the testicles to drop back to their original position. Seek qualified medical attention as soon as possible.

5. Testicle Revival (kicking to sacrum)

This procedure is used to treat a patient whose testicles have been kicked up into his pelvis. It is not used to restore breathing. Place the patient in a sitting position and stand behind him. Lightly kick the sacrum in the center of the hips, with the ball or sole of your foot. This may cause the testicles to drop back to their original position. Do not kick too forcefully or you may damage the sacral spine. Two methods of supporting the upper body are shown. In the first method, place your hands on the patients shoulders (see 5A). In the second method, lift one armpit, slightly elevating one buttock (see 5B).

  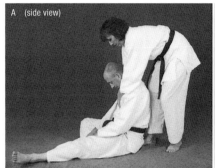 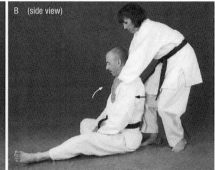

1. Knee-to-Spine Revival

2. Spine-Slap Revival

GV-26
(philtrum)
In center of groove below nose, slightly above the midpoint.

3.1 Acupoint Revival (press GV-26)

LI-4
(backhand)
Center of muscle in web of thumb, slightly toward 2nd metacarpal. Do not press if pregnant.

3.2 Acupoint Revival (press LI-4)

KI-1
(sole of foot)
In recess 1/3 the distance from from base of toes to heel.

3.3 Acupoint Revival (press KI-1)

4. Testicle Revival (lifting and dropping)

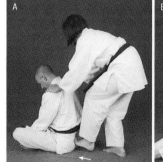 

5. Testicle Revival (kicking to sacrum)

How you stand and how you move are the basic building blocks of martial techniques. They are the key factors which make a specific technique, such as a hold or throw, possible. Different martial arts are often distinguished by preferences for certain types of foot and body positions, and certain methods of locomotion. Some styles prefer linear motions, some styles prefer circular motions, some blend the two together. In some arts, motions are free-flowing and continuous; in others they are abrupt, precise, and rigidly defined.

STANCES + MOVEMENT

In Hapkido, stances are an integral part of continuous movement. Hapkido self-defense technique is characterized by a constant flow of striking, blocking, holding, and throwing techniques executed from highly mobile stances—from balanced or unbalanced postures. Hapkido footwork and body movement is continuous and often incorporates linear, circular, or spinning movements to generate power or blend with an opponent's force. The following pages show common stances and briefly discuss the basic forms of Hapkido movement.

Overview

In any martial art, stances are defined by specific positions of the body and feet. These positions are normally used to execute specific techniques, or may become the linking points in a continuous movement. When body and feet relationships vary beyond certain defined limits, a "stance change" is said to have occurred.

Traditionally, stances in many martial arts were rigidly defined in terms of their purpose, body-foot placement, and weight distribution. Arts such as Karate viewed the stance as a "firmly rooted foundation" from which all techniques were executed. The emphasis was on "stability," which was expressed in the analogy, "a tree which bends but does not topple." Over time, as fighting technique evolved (and trees were chopped down), firmly rooted stances became obsolete, as an increased emphasis on mobility was stressed in those arts involved in competition, combat, and practical self-defense.

Hapkido Stance-Movement Theory

In Hapkido, mobility is deemed more important than stability. Movement is constant until a situation is resolved. Techniques are executed while moving or during a brief pause in movement, from either balanced or unbalanced positions. This occurs from standing, falling, seated, and reclining positions. As a result, one cannot conceptualize Hapkido stances as specifically defined formations from which one operates. Stances are better thought of as one part of an overall concept of continuous movement. It is usually more helpful to think of Hapkido stances as the body and feet positions from which a particular technique is executed, or as the links in a continuous series of movements or techniques.

The diversity of Hapkido's stances and movements are illustrated by the following example. If you are knocked off balance by an opponent's strike you may either: 1) attempt to recover your balance and counter or 2) use your off-balance movement to generate a counter (see photos).

The stances associated with these two scenarios are obviously quite different. Naturally, anyone would prefer to counter from a strong base designed to optimize technique; however, you may not be able to recover your balance, or if you do, the time required may create additional risk. The second scenario (i.e., kicking while falling) is more efficient in that it utilizes existing movement to generate a counter technique. The body and foot placement associated with the second scenario may not typically be thought of as a stance per se, but that is exactly what it is.

Hapkido makes use of *any available position* to execute offensive or defensive techniques. Consequently, it is very difficult to define all the stances that might be used in executing Hapkido techniques. The stances that follow are best thought of as the *optimal* feet and body positions for a range of techniques—but not the only ones. In Hapkido one practices techniques from a variety of both balanced and unbalanced postures.

Hapkido Stances

Hapkido's stances were mostly developed to maximize speed and power while camouflaging intent. This chapter describes 22 common stances, organized into three basic categories: relaxed stances, fighting stances, and traditional stances.

Relaxed Stances

Relaxed stances resemble everyday standing or sitting postures. Hapkido makes significant use of relaxed stances to camouflage tactics and lure an opponent into a false sense of security. Attacking and defending from relaxed stances is also useful when one wishes to maintain a low profile or minimize disturbance to people nearby. When relaxed stances are used in conjunction with certain strikes and holds, it is possible to disguise the fact that any martial arts skills are involved. For professionals involved in personnel protection, security, and law enforcement, this can be indispensible, if not a political and occupational necessity. In most Hapkido systems, reacting and applying self-defense techniques from relaxed stances is one of the first skills the student will learn.

Hapkido stances are an integral part of continuous movement (sequence shows one person striking two opponents)

Striking from a balanced stance

Fighting Stances

In fighting stances, the position of the hands, feet, and body is optimized to facilitate execution of techniques. When you adopt a fighting stance you signal to your opponent (and anyone else watching) that you are prepared to fight. If you don't want them to know, don't adopt a fighting stance. If "excessive force" becomes a legal issue, everyone will remember your display of expertise all the more vividly.

The manner in which a stance is adopted can signal aggression, confidence, indifference, or fear. Psychological manipulation of an opponent can be an important component of obtaining an advantage. If you can intimidate your opponent from the onset, fighting may not even be necessary. Conversely, an opponent's stance can tell you a lot about what that person is likely to do. Issues of camouflage or surprise aside, fighting stances are usually favored for launching both offensive and defensive techniques, since the body can be optimally positioned.

Traditional Stances

A number of traditional stances are no longer favored by most Hapkido practitioners in actual fighting. While they were extremely effective in their day, constant improvements in fighting techniques have rendered them obsolete. Nonetheless, they are still valuable as tools for teaching body movement, balance, and coordination. Learning traditional stances

and movements also provides a useful foundation of skills, of distinct advantage when improvising or creating new techniques. The study and practice of traditional forms is also helpful to understanding Hapkido's origins. Traditional stances can also to be appreciated for their aesthetic value, which makes them well suited for demonstrations.

Other Stances

Hapkido is a very diverse style. Many masters have adopted or created stances other than those shown in this chapter. Many schools do not even teach specific stances, but instead focus on movement or footwork associated with specific techniques. This chapter is not intended to be an authoritative listing of all stances in use, but an outline of those most commonly observed in Hapkido training. All stances shown are freely modified in practical self-defense to create innumerable variations.

Offense vs. Defense

Any stance can be used to launch offensive or defensive actions, although they tend to be more suited to one or the other. This will be discussed in detail on the following pages. Historically, most Hapkido systems preferred right-lead stances (right foot forward), since this was thought to favor defensive actions (for a right-handed person); whereas left-lead stances were thought to favor offensive actions. Generally, you should practice techniques from both leads, since this allows you to respond instinctively to any situation.

The following terms are widely used within the martial arts world to classify stances. Although these terms are not commonly used in Hapkido, understanding how stances relate to specific skills is important when analyzing an opponent's tactics and probable range of techniques.

Strong Lead – Weak Lead

Strong or weak lead defines how an opponent's strength is placed relative to you. In a *weak-lead* fighting stance, the weak side is in front (leads) and the strong side is in the rear. In a right-handed person this would mean placing the left hand and foot forward. In theory, this favors using the rear hand and foot for attacking. This stance is often used in Western boxing, where the left hand sets up and the right hand is used for power.

In a *strong-lead* fighting stance, the strong side is in front (leads) and the weak side is in the rear. In a right-handed person this would mean placing the right hand and foot forward. In theory, this favors techniques using the front hand and foot. An example can be seen in certain Chinese styles in which the lead hand is used for striking and the rear hand for feinting or blocking.

Open Stance – Closed Stance

Open or closed stance defines how an opponent's targets are placed relative to you. In an open stance the targets of the head and body appear *open* to the opponent. An open stance exists when one person is leading with the left side and the other is leading with the right. In a closed stance the targets of the head and body appear *closed* to the opponent. A closed stance exists when both persons lead with the same side (e.g., right lead).

Striking from an unbalanced stance (while falling)

Relaxed Stance

Fighting Stance

Traditional Stance

STANCE SUMMARY

Stance	Balance	Comments
Relaxed Stances		
1 Relaxed Standing Stance	Equal	Basic stance; non-confrontational; also called natural stance.
2 Relaxed Cat Stance	70–90% back foot	Ready stance; non-confrontational.
3 Relaxed Walking Stance	Constantly changing	Offensive moving stance; highly mobile; good disguise for strikes.
4 Cowering Stance	50–60% back foot	Defensive stance; highly mobile; good disguise for strikes and back kicks.
5 Relaxed Seated Stance	Equal	Defensive stance; used with seated defense techniques.
Fighting Stances		
6 Front Stance	50–60% front foot	Powerful striking stance; very stable; low mobility.
7 Short Front Stance	50–60% front foot	Basic fighting stance; highly mobile; good for fast kick attacks or counters.
8 45° Front Stance	50–60% front foot	Basic fighting stance; well protected; good for turning counters.
9 Side Stance	Equal	Good stance for side kicks or turning kicks; poor lateral mobility.
10 Back Stance	50–75% back foot	Basic defensive stance; good balance between stability and mobility.
11 Cat Stance	70–90% back foot	Very flexible; good for close-in fighting; poor stability, good mobility.
12 Open Hand Stance	50–70% back foot	Used against weapons, or with holding and throwing techniques.
13 Grappling Stance	Equal	Used when grappling, holding, and throwing.
14 Two Knee Stance	Equal	Used for ground fighting and grappling.
15 One Knee Stance	Equal	Used for ground fighting and grappling.
16 Seated Guard	Equal	Used for ground fighting against standing opponent; good for kicks and throws.
Traditional Stances		
17 Fists at Side	75% back foot	Rarely used traditional free fighting stance; often against low attacks.
18 Hands Overhead	75–90% back foot	Rarely used traditional Cat Stance; often against multiple attackers, or to appear tall.
19 Knife Hands High	50–75% back foot	Traditional Back Stance; often used against knife, or to appear taller than reality.
20 Knife Hands Low	50–75% back foot	Traditional Back Stance; often used against knife or sword.
21 Folded Arms	75–90% back foot	Traditional Cat Stance; often used to disguise intent or hide hands.
22 Front Horse	Equal	Rarely used traditional stance; often used to appear larger.

Twenty-two common Hapkido stances are summarized at left and shown below. These stances are shown in greater detail in the author's 1136-page Hapkido book.

1. Relaxed Standing Stance

2. Relaxed Cat Stance

3. Relaxed Walking Stance

4. Cowering Stance

5. Relaxed Seated Stance

6. Front Stance

7. Short Front Stance

8. 45° Front Stance

9. Side Stance

10. Back Stance

11. Cat Stance

12. Open Hand Stance

13. Grappling Stance

14. Two Knee Stance

15. One Knee Stance

16. Seated Guard

17. Fists at Side

18. Hands Overhead

19. Knife Hands High

20. Knife Hands Low

21. Folded Arms

22. Front Horse

Overview

As previously stated, Hapkido self-defense technique is characterized by a constant flow of striking, blocking, holding, and throwing techniques executed from highly mobile stances—from balanced or unbalanced postures. Hapkido footwork and body movement is continuous and often incorporates linear, circular, or spinning movements to generate power or blend with an opponent's force. Constant changes in body positioning and the rhythm of attack are designed to make targeting difficult while disorienting and frustrating your opponent. The Hapkidoist's center of gravity is always shifting between one and two feet, depending upon an attacker's movement or the techniques to be executed.

To the uneducated observer, Hapkido movements often appear awkward, ungainly or out of control when compared to other martial arts. However, this is a function of Hapkido's unique and practical nature. Hapkido was not designed to be pretty or have spectator appeal. It was designed to work in self-defense or combat situations. Its techniques and movements are entirely based upon this reality; aesthetics are irrelevant. Hapkido's form perfectly follows its function. Its movements are designed to be *deceptive* and *irregular,* to camouflage tactics, techniques, and skill-level. Moreover, Hapkido even uses *unbalanced* conditions (falls or mistakes) to generate counters.

It is not uncommon to hear Hapkido movement described as anything from "a tornado with arms and legs flying in all directions" to "a passive insignificant movement with decisive results." It is also sometimes characterized as misleading, sneaky, or dirty fighting. In reality, it is none of these things and all of these things.

The broad range of contradictory observations point to both its eclectic nature and broad range of movement possibilities. Self-defense examples demonstrating Hapkido's *constant movement* principle are shown at right.

Purpose of Movement

In Hapkido, the purpose of movement is to optimize the body's placement with respect to your opponent's. Specific movements are used to facilitate execution of offensive or defensive technique, or to remove one's self from harm's way. All forms of movement, regardless of posture or form of locomotion, possess the same objectives:

- Avoid an attack
- Launch an attack or counterattack
- Maximize the efficiency of techniques
- Disrupt the opponent's tactics
- Create an opening in opponent's defense
- Create flaws in opponent's movements

Types of Movement

Hapkido movement occurs from any possible position, and is characterized by stepping, sliding, running, walking, jumping, turning, spinning, crawling, dragging, rolling, and tumbling. There are about 71 basic forms of movement divided into three categories: Standing Movement, Ground Movement, and Transitional Movement.

Standing movement is characterized by foot locomotion from a standing position. Ground movement uses any part of the body for locomotion, from a reclining, sitting, or kneeling position. Transitional movement is used to change between standing and ground positions. In Hapkido, standing and ground movements are not thought of separately, but as a single integrated concept of motion. Basic forms of locomotion used in standing, ground, and transitional movements are outlined on the following pages. In practical self-defense, these basic movements are freely modified based on tactics and technique, leading to innumerable possibilities.

Standing Movement

Ground Movement

Transitional Movement

Constant movement from a standing position, against two opponents (note the turns and body spins between strikes; the constant change of position; one move flows into another).

Constant ground movement from a reclining position against four opponents (note the body pivots and rolls between strikes; positions constantly change; one move flows into another).

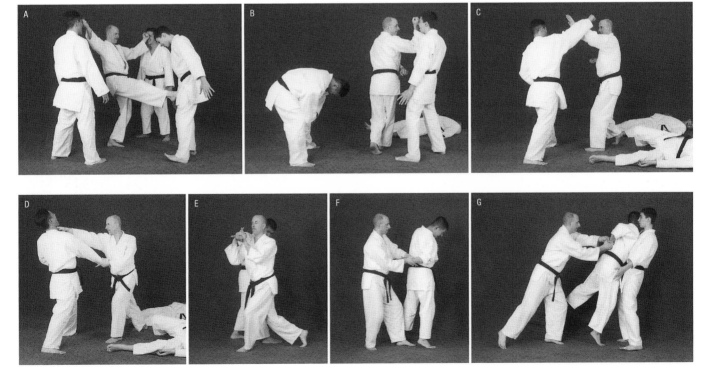

Constant movement against four attackers: triple strike (A); cross-step and strike (B); 270° pivot, block, strike (C–D); 180° pivot under arm, hammer lock, throw into attacker (E–G).

1. Forward Step

2. Forward Slide

3. Forward Shuffle

4. Back Step

5. Back Slide

6. Back Shuffle

7. Side Step–Front Pivot (left)

8. Side Step–Front Pivot (right)

9. Side Step–Back Pivot (left)

10. Side Step–Back Pivot (right)

11. Side Slide (front left)

12. Side Slide (front right)

13. Side Slide (back left)

14. Side Slide (back right)

15. Side Slide–Step (left)

16. Side Slide–Step (right)

17. Turn Step (face forward)

18. Turn Step (face behind)

19. Pivot (face side)

20. Pivot (face behind)

Almost all standing footwork in Hapkido derives from about 40 basic steps, which are combined or altered to create innumerable possibilities. Photos, further explanation, and practical applications are found in the author's 1136-page Hapkido book.

Outlined feet indicate start position; *solid* feet indicate ending. Numbers indicate which foot moves first.

P	Pivot
B	Back Foot
F	Front Foot
1, 2	Sequence

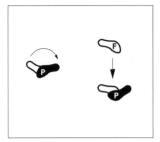

21. Step-Pivot (front step)

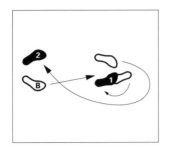

26. Rear Draw Turning

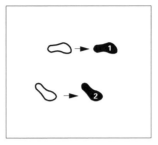

31. Forward Shuffle

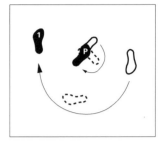

36. Forward Turn (right pivot)

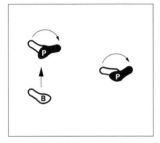

22. Step-Pivot (back step)

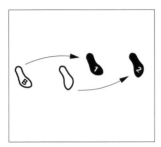

27. Cross Step Behind

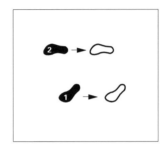

32. Back Shuffle

37. Back Turn (left pivot)

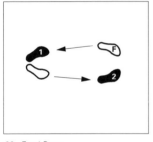

23. Front Draw

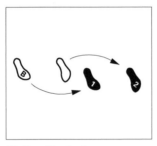

28. Cross Step Front

33. Side Shuffle

38. Back Turn (right pivot)

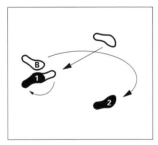

24. Front Draw Turning

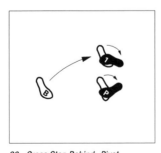

29. Cross Step Behind–Pivot

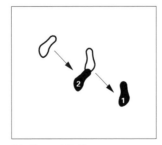

34. Diagonal Shuffle

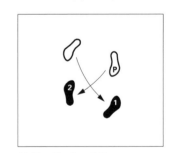

39. Two Step Turn (left)

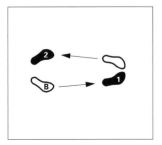

25. Rear Draw

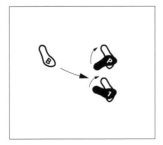

30. Cross Step Front–Pivot

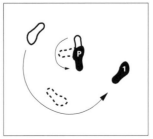

35. Forward Turn (left pivot)

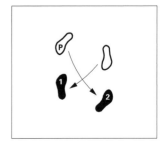

40. Two Step Turn (right)

Ground Movement

In Hapkido, various forms of ground movement can be executed from a kneeling, sitting, or reclining position against one or more opponents operating from any position, including airborne, standing, sitting, or reclining. As with standing technique, specific movements are used to facilitate execution of offensive or defensive techniques, or to remove oneself from the area of confrontation. Ground movement could become necessary for any of the following reasons:

• You have been thrown
• You have tripped or fallen
• You are executing a sacrifice technique
• You are surprised while seated or resting

• You cannot stand due to foot/leg damage
• You cannot stand due to restricted space
• You need to remain low to avoid hazards (e.g., gunfire, explosions, machinery)
• You have been restrained or tied up
• You prefer to fight on the ground

In this book, ground movements are classified according to method of locomotion. There are approximately eleven basic types of movement, which are shown below and on the opposite page. Some of these movements are quite common, for instance, Shoulder Rolls; others are rarely used except when linked to specific techniques and objectives, for instance, the Crab Walk or Side Crawl. Detailed explanations of each technique can

Practicing shoulder rolls for height and distance

be found in the author's 1136-page Hapkido book. This larger work also includes a section on "transitional movement," which are techniques typically used to make a transition from a standing position to the ground, or from a ground position to a standing posture.

1. Knee Walk

2. Knee-Foot Walk

3. Knee-Hand Drag

4. Crab Walk

5. Monkey Walk

6. Buttock Pivot

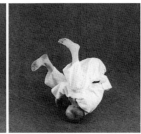

7. Forward Shoulder Roll

8. Back Shoulder Roll

9. Forward Roll

10. Side Roll

11. Side Crawl

Breakfalls

If you do not know how to fall, most throws will produce serious injuries. A *breakfall* is a specific method of falling, designed to protect your body from damage as you hit the ground. This involves specific formations of your body which minimize impact by dispersing force over a large surface area. Eight basic types of breakfalls are commonly used in Hapkido. They are shown below and on the next page, and should be learned from a qualified instructor to avoid injuries. The breakfall you will use is based on how you are thrown. In all breakfalls, you will attempt to control your body position while airborne. As your body lands in the proper position, you will *slap* and *Kihap* (energy-shout) at the same time. The photo at the end of each sequence, shows each breakfall being used during a typical throwing technique. The *Throws* chapter of the author's 1136-page Hapkido book contains a complete description of each breakfall, along with basic throwing principles and 132 typical Hapkido throws.

The Slap

In most breakfalls you will slap with your hand and forearm to distribute the force of impact. This also helps to position your body, and assists in timing. The force of your slap must be adjusted, based on the hardness of the surface you are falling onto. While it is common to see students endlessly practicing forceful slaps on the mat, these same slaps will cause you to injure or break your hand when falling on hard surfaces like concrete.

The Kihap

A *Kihap* is an abrupt shout designed to focus your energy and power. In breakfalls, it helps protect the body from injury, keeps the wind from being knocked out of your lungs, and causes your body to naturally relax on impact.

Self-Initiated Breakfalls

One of Hapkido's distinct qualities is that you will often initiate your own fall, in order to counter joint locks or throws. This saves your joints from serious injury, and propels you ahead of a thrower's force. Self-initiated falls are the basis of many counters and escapes.

1. Front Fall

2. Soft Front Fall

3. Back Fall

4. Bridge Fall

5. Sit-Out Side Fall

6. Sweep Side Fall

7. Flip Side Fall

8. Twisting Side Fall

Attack points are the specific parts of your body (hands, feet, elbows, knees, head, etc.) which are used to attack specific targets and execute specific techniques. The method of attack is usually a strike; however, these same body surfaces are often used when applying joint locks, chokes, throws, and pins. The use of a particular attack point usually involves specific formations of the hand, foot, or other parts of the body. Most Hapkido systems make use of about sixty primary attack points, which are shown on the following pages.

ATTACK POINTS + TARGETS

Hapkido training also includes study of human anatomy. Detailed knowledge of pressure points is used to magnify the effect of strikes or holds, or to accelerate the healing of injuries. The illustrations on subsequent pages show the basic pressure point targets commonly used in Hapkido; many others are also used. However, location, function, and use of these basic acupoints should be learned before proceeding further. Remember, it is better to become highly proficient in a few techniques, than marginally competent with many.

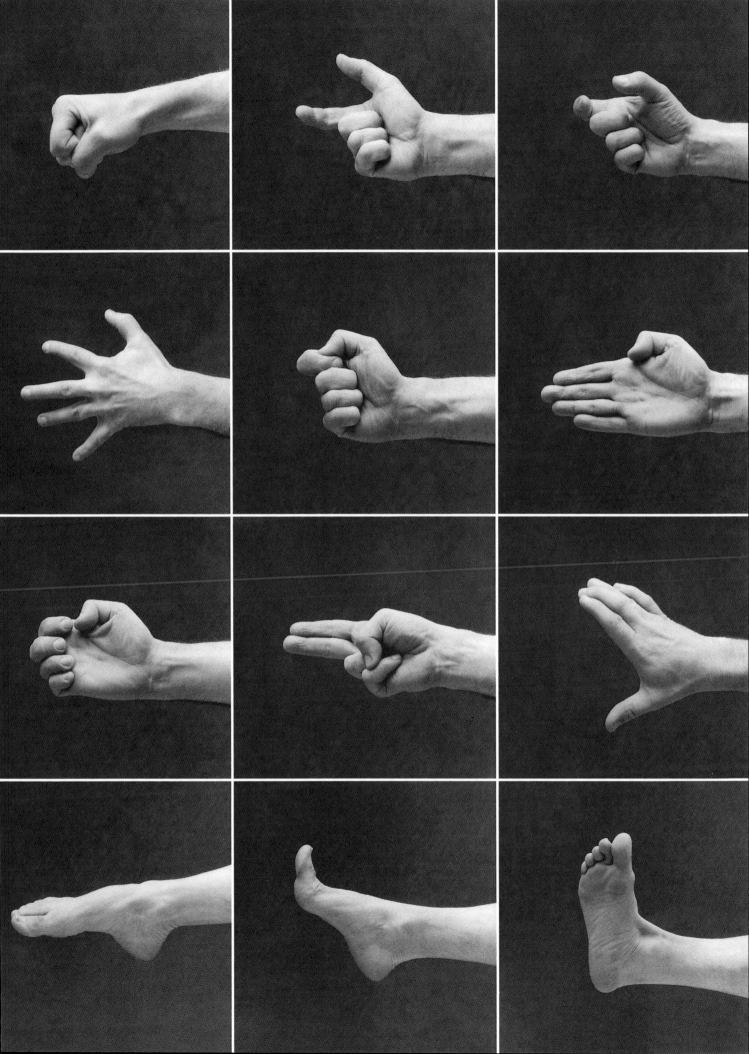

1. Fore Fist

2. Back Fist

3. Hammer Fist

4. Loose Hammer Fist

5. Ki Hammer Fist

6. Thumb Fist

7. Middle Finger Fist

8. Index Finger Fist

9. Knuckle Fist

10. Knuckle Hand

11. Knife Hand

12. Cutting Hand

13. Relaxed Back Hand

14. Tense Back Hand

15. Ki Back Hand

16. Spear Hand

17. Spear Hand – 2 Fingers

18. Spear Hand – 2 Fingers

19. Spear Hand – 1 Finger

20. Ridge Hand

21. Ox Jaw Hand

22. Chicken Hand

23. Tiger Mouth Hand

24. Palm Heel Hand

25. Open Hand

26. Bear Hand

27. Claw Hand

28. Five Fingertip Hand

29. Thumb Hand

30. Pincer Hand

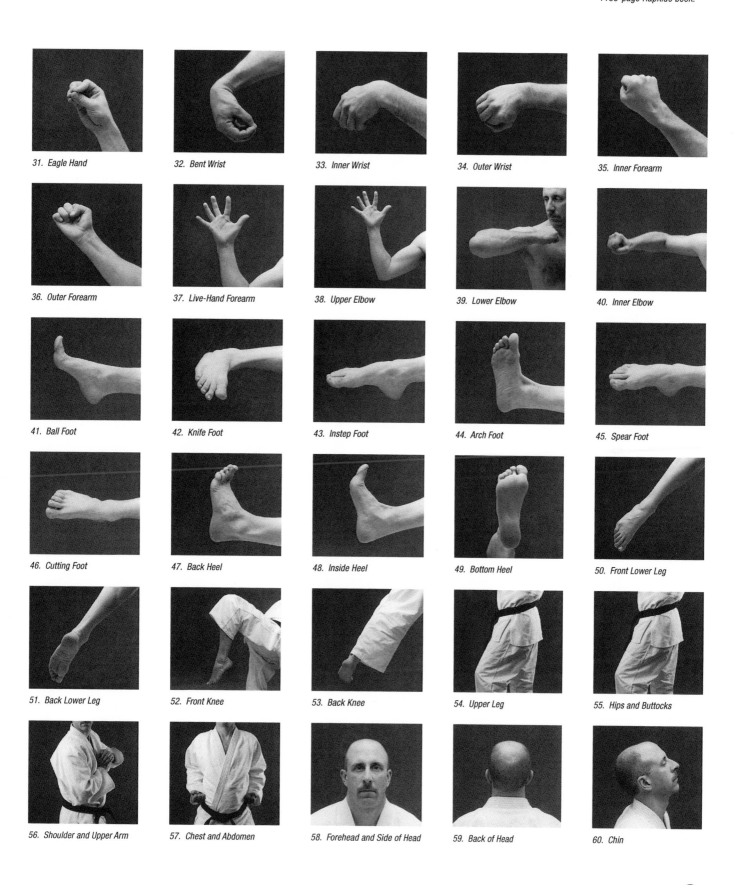

31. Eagle Hand

32. Bent Wrist

33. Inner Wrist

34. Outer Wrist

35. Inner Forearm

36. Outer Forearm

37. Live-Hand Forearm

38. Upper Elbow

39. Lower Elbow

40. Inner Elbow

41. Ball Foot

42. Knife Foot

43. Instep Foot

44. Arch Foot

45. Spear Foot

46. Cutting Foot

47. Back Heel

48. Inside Heel

49. Bottom Heel

50. Front Lower Leg

51. Back Lower Leg

52. Front Knee

53. Back Knee

54. Upper Leg

55. Hips and Buttocks

56. Shoulder and Upper Arm

57. Chest and Abdomen

58. Forehead and Side of Head

59. Back of Head

60. Chin

PRESSURE POINT TARGETS

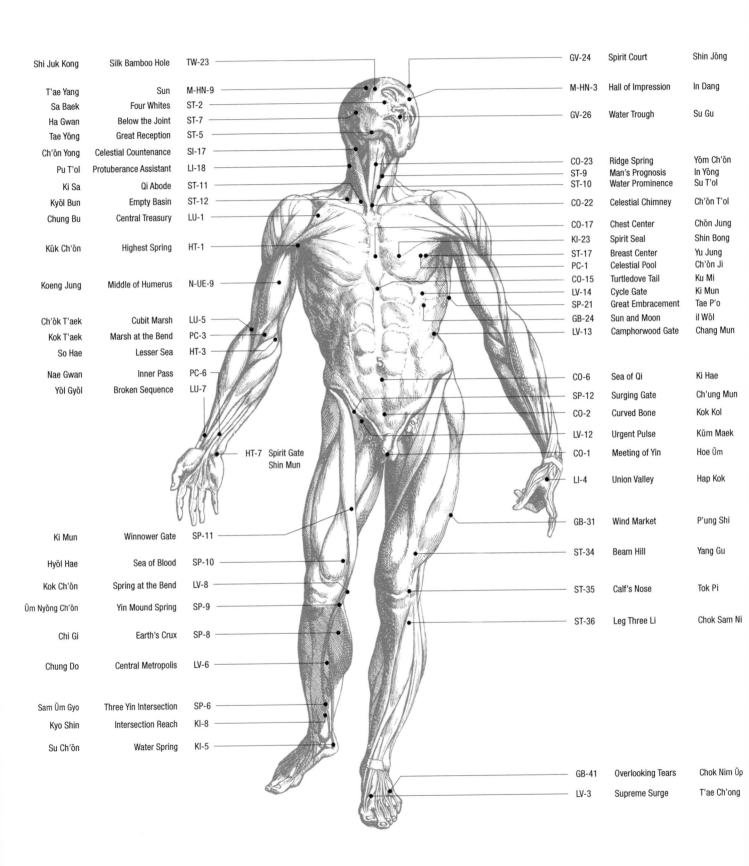

Shi Juk Kong	Silk Bamboo Hole	TW-23
T'ae Yang	Sun	M-HN-9
Sa Baek	Four Whites	ST-2
Ha Gwan	Below the Joint	ST-7
Tae Yŏng	Great Reception	ST-5
Ch'ŏn Yong	Celestial Countenance	SI-17
Pu T'ol	Protuberance Assistant	LI-18
Ki Sa	Qi Abode	ST-11
Kyŏl Bun	Empty Basin	ST-12
Chung Bu	Central Treasury	LU-1
Kŭk Ch'ŏn	Highest Spring	HT-1
Koeng Jung	Middle of Humerus	N-UE-9
Ch'ŏk T'aek	Cubit Marsh	LU-5
Kok T'aek	Marsh at the Bend	PC-3
So Hae	Lesser Sea	HT-3
Nae Gwan	Inner Pass	PC-6
Yŏl Gyŏl	Broken Sequence	LU-7

HT-7   Spirit Gate
Shin Mun

Ki Mun	Winnower Gate	SP-11
Hyŏl Hae	Sea of Blood	SP-10
Kok Ch'ŏn	Spring at the Bend	LV-8
Ŭm Nyŏng Ch'ŏn	Yin Mound Spring	SP-9
Chi Gi	Earth's Crux	SP-8
Chung Do	Central Metropolis	LV-6
Sam Ŭm Gyo	Three Yin Intersection	SP-6
Kyo Shin	Intersection Reach	KI-8
Su Ch'ŏn	Water Spring	KI-5

GV-24	Spirit Court	Shin Jŏng
M-HN-3	Hall of Impression	In Dang
GV-26	Water Trough	Su Gu
CO-23	Ridge Spring	Yŏm Ch'ŏn
ST-9	Man's Prognosis	In Yŏng
ST-10	Water Prominence	Su T'ol
CO-22	Celestial Chimney	Ch'ŏn T'ol
CO-17	Chest Center	Chŏn Jung
KI-23	Spirit Seal	Shin Bong
ST-17	Breast Center	Yu Jung
PC-1	Celestial Pool	Ch'ŏn Ji
CO-15	Turtledove Tail	Ku Mi
LV-14	Cycle Gate	Ki Mun
SP-21	Great Embracement	Tae P'o
GB-24	Sun and Moon	il Wŏl
LV-13	Camphorwood Gate	Chang Mun
CO-6	Sea of Qi	Ki Hae
SP-12	Surging Gate	Ch'ung Mun
CO-2	Curved Bone	Kok Kol
LV-12	Urgent Pulse	Kŭm Maek
CO-1	Meeting of Yin	Hoe Ŭm
LI-4	Union Valley	Hap Kok
GB-31	Wind Market	P'ung Shi
ST-34	Beam Hill	Yang Gu
ST-35	Calf's Nose	Tok Pi
ST-36	Leg Three Li	Chok Sam Ni
GB-41	Overlooking Tears	Chok Nim Ŭp
LV-3	Supreme Surge	T'ae Ch'ong

56

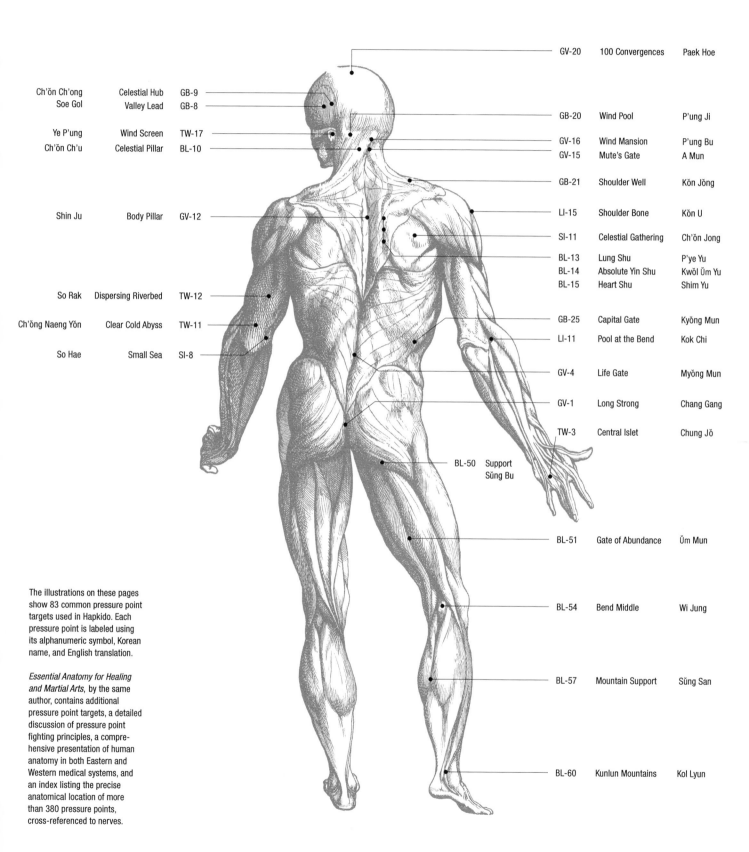

GV-20   100 Convergences   Paek Hoe

Ch'ŏn Ch'ong   Celestial Hub   GB-9
Soe Gol   Valley Lead   GB-8

GB-20   Wind Pool   P'ung Ji

Ye P'ung   Wind Screen   TW-17
Ch'ŏn Ch'u   Celestial Pillar   BL-10

GV-16   Wind Mansion   P'ung Bu
GV-15   Mute's Gate   A Mun

GB-21   Shoulder Well   Kŏn Jŏng

Shin Ju   Body Pillar   GV-12

LI-15   Shoulder Bone   Kŏn U

SI-11   Celestial Gathering   Ch'ŏn Jong

BL-13   Lung Shu   P'ye Yu
BL-14   Absolute Yin Shu   Kwŏl Ŭm Yu
BL-15   Heart Shu   Shim Yu

So Rak   Dispersing Riverbed   TW-12

GB-25   Capital Gate   Kyŏng Mun

Ch'ŏng Naeng Yŏn   Clear Cold Abyss   TW-11

LI-11   Pool at the Bend   Kok Chi

So Hae   Small Sea   SI-8

GV-4   Life Gate   Myŏng Mun

GV-1   Long Strong   Chang Gang

TW-3   Central Islet   Chung Jŏ

BL-50   Support   Sŭng Bu

BL-51   Gate of Abundance   Ŭm Mun

The illustrations on these pages show 83 common pressure point targets used in Hapkido. Each pressure point is labeled using its alphanumeric symbol, Korean name, and English translation.

Essential Anatomy for Healing and Martial Arts, by the same author, contains additional pressure point targets, a detailed discussion of pressure point fighting principles, a comprehensive presentation of human anatomy in both Eastern and Western medical systems, and an index listing the precise anatomical location of more than 380 pressure points, cross-referenced to nerves.

BL-54   Bend Middle   Wi Jung

BL-57   Mountain Support   Sŭng San

BL-60   Kunlun Mountains   Kol Lyun

Overview

Part Two of this book provided a brief overview of the basic elements which compose Hapkido. In the author's larger book, more than 1000 basic strikes, blocks, holds, and throws, among other skills, are shown. Part Three of this book describes how these basic techniques are combined for use in combat or self-defense. This is the essence of Hapkido's physical side, and what really distinguishes it from other martial arts—namely, its ability to blend all the major forms of martial technique into a unified whole.

There are two basic modes from which Hapkido techniques are commonly executed: attacking and counterattacking. In attacking, you will decide when to initiate an offensive action. In counterattacking, you will respond based upon your opponent's actions. Most combat is essentially a blending of these two basic modes, with combatants shifting between offensive and defensive actions.

Attacking

This is the art of seizing opportunity first. An offensive action can consist of a strike, hold, or throw—or a blend of techniques. In Hapkido, attacks are launched either by feinting to set up the attack, or by blitzing.

Blitzing

Blitzing involves catching your opponent by surprise, before they can respond. Blitzing attacks are usually launched from a relaxed stance to camouflage your intentions. Blitzing attacks are often used when you know you cannot avoid a fight, and wish to seize the advantage by attacking first. This is often prudent when confronting much larger opponents or multiple attackers. It is also possible to blitz from fighting stances.

Feinting

When attacking, feinting is used to create an opening for a particular technique that might otherwise be blocked or countered. A common offensive feint is to make a striking motion with your lead hand or leg, and attack with your rear. Feints are also called fakes.

Counterattacking

In counterattacking, you will respond based upon your opponent's actions. You may react to an attack by executing a block, strike, hold, or throw—or by responding with a combination of techniques (sequential or simultaneous). In Hapkido, counterattacks are launched either by feinting to draw a specific attack, or by reacting to an unknown attack. Specific self-defense responses to specific forms of attack will be organized and presented as follows. This is how the art of Hapkido is commonly structured and taught:

Self-Defense Techniques
- Defense Against Punches
- Defense Against Kicks
- Defense Against Holds
- Defense Against Chokes
- Defense Against Joint Locks
- Defense Against Throws
- Ground Defenses
- Defense Using One or No Arms

Attacking Techniques
- Offensive Strikes
- Offensive Holds
- Offensive Throws

Special Circumstances
- Defense Against Multiple Opponents
- Protecting Another Person (not shown, see the author's 1136-page book)

Self-Defense techniques involving weapons are briefly covered in Part 4 of this book.

Hapkido's Unique Approach

In its essence, Hapkido is an art of great versatility with many options for addressing a situation. You can attack first, or wait until threatened. You can respond with devastating destruction, or be merciful and gentle. You can respond by emphasizing a particular technique area, such as holds, or flow freely between strikes, blocks, holds, and throws, in any order you wish. There are no rigid guidelines. The choices are yours, and should be governed by a sense of morality, compassion, and appropriateness.

Personalizing Technique

How you choose to combine technique is ultimately a matter of choice. Self-defense responses are never determined by following rigid guidelines, but by responding to the unique dynamics of a situation as it unfolds, and by understanding the limitations of your own body. This means knowing the limits of your technique, and evolving technique that suits your physique. We are all built differently, each of us possessing specific strengths and weaknesses. You must find those techniques that are most suited to your own unique physical qualities. If a combination you are practicing feels clumsy, determine if your mechanics are at fault (maybe you just need to practice it more), or if the technique itself is inappropriate for you. Remember, this is the body you were born with. You can only modify your physical structure within certain limits. Accept who you are. Build on your assets. Strengthen and protect your weaknesses.

Blitzing Attack: Catching opponent unaware

Counterattack: Avoiding a kick and striking inner leg

Multiple Options

Hapkido is an art consisting of thousands of techniques. The purpose of so many techniques is not to confound you, but to provide options. Life's situations are infinitely variable; combat is always changing; human physiques can be very diverse. No martial arts system can hope to embrace so many variables unless it possesses *great flexibility* in application. Hapkido attempts to address this reality by providing options. It is not essential that you become equally proficient in every strike, block, hold, and throw practiced in Hapkido, but rather that you find things you do well, and evolve a method for combining these techniques that suits your physique and moral temperament.

Varying The Level of Force

Hapkido techniques can be executed using various levels of force. To make a technique more gentle: strike non-vital targets, hit lightly, use pain to control movement, apply holds carefully, and avoid techniques that lead to serious injuries (e.g., eye strikes, joint breaks, neck twists, spine strikes). Most throws can be devastating if an opponent does not know how to fall. To make a throw more gentle: reduce velocity, eliminate joint locks, and control an opponent's body position as they hit the ground. Guide them to a safe landing, protecting their head, spine, and shoulder from serious impact. Conversely, you can seriously injure even a skilled opponent by manipulating the fall, so that they hit their head or land on their shoulder or lower back.

An impractical kick is practical in the right situation

Improvisation

Improvisation is the hallmark of a skilled Hapkidoist. The most effective martial artists are those who respond intuitively to the changing dynamics of combat—improvising and applying techniques as required. Practice the basic combinations you are taught, or make up your own. Drill constantly so that these movements become ingrained in you. This is the basis of improvisation: building a vocabulary of elements which you will *instinctively* select at the appropriate time. After you have memorized these things, stop thinking about them and allow your mind-body to make the choices and connections it deems most appropriate. This same approach is used when teaching improvisation in music.

When learning new techniques, do not become dogmatic about using them exactly as they were shown to you. This only leads to stagnation and encourages mindlessness. Use what you are taught as a starting point. Once you grasp basic concepts and methods of application, feel free to adapt, improvise, or create your own techniques—based on the technical principles covered in the *Hapkido Philosophy* chapter, and the core techniques that define Hapkido. Improvise based on the flow of combat, not your desire to use this or that technique. Find those things that work for you, and build on them.

Determining What is Practical

This is an area of great controversy, and often stirs heated debates about the relative merits of this technique versus that. These questions are not easily resolved. So much depends upon how two combatants match-up, and how their styles mesh. Many superior fighters are beaten by inferior opponents with inferior techniques, because they were totally unfamiliar with the opponents' style or method of fighting. Size, weight, speed, the physical environment, and emotional states all influence the outcome of a confrontation. The techniques you feel are most impractical may be exactly that—impractical in *most* situations. However, in certain unusual circumstances, they might provide your best

or only response. For example, attempting to block a hand strike with a Crescent Kick (a traditional defense) is usually far too slow to be practical. However, if your arms are restrained behind your back (or broken), it may be your *only* response (see lower-left).

Every technique possesses limitations, some more than others. When confronted with a technique which seems useless, remember, someone went to a great deal of trouble to create it, pass it down, and teach it. Perhaps there are benefits you do not yet perceive. Rather than focusing on its limitations, try to determine when it would be most useful.

When you are learning new techniques, try to keep an open mind. It is very easy to form initial opinions that you will come to change later on. The simple truth is, any technique can work if you do it well enough, set it up properly, and use it in an appropriate situation. As time goes by, popular consensus regarding preferred techniques always changes. Remember, the worst technique will work if you do it well; the best technique will fail if you do it poorly.

Techniques Shown in this Book

The techniques shown in the third part of this book are representative of Hapkido's basic approach to various self-defense situations. These techniques were selected from the 600-plus techniques documented in the author's 1136-page Hapkido book. These techniques are not meant to represent any particular style or school, but to reflect the art as a whole, defining *what Hapkido is,* and *what it is becoming.*

The 600-plus techniques shown in the larger book were selected based on practicality as well as concerns for preserving certain historical qualities unique to Hapkido. Consequently, the techniques reflect both traditional and modern approaches. Be aware that there are literally thousands of possible responses to any given situation. It is beyond the scope of any text to document all of these numerous possibilities.

In Hapkido, strikes are countered using a blend of counterstrikes, holds, and throws. Technique selection and sequence is entirely up to the user. Regardless of how you attempt to counter a strike, you must first commit one of the following actions: block and counterstrike, block and apply a hold, or block and apply a throw (block means to block or avoid). Any of these three initial responses can be followed by additional strikes, holds, or throws, in any order you wish, as circumstances dictate. The following pages show six typical

DEFENSE AGAINST PUNCHES

techniques, which are organized based on the initial defensive response employed: strike, kick, hold, or throw. Although these counters are typically called "Defenses Against Punches," these defenses can be applied against any form of hand strike, a push, or an attempt to grab. In its entirety, this Hapkido category of self-defense consists of many, many techniques. The author's 1136-page Hapkido book contains 120 typical defenses against punches, along with closeups and a detailed presentation of basic principles.

1. Block and Strike

A. Defend from Relaxed Stance
B. L Inside Block
C. R Inside Elbow Strike

As attacker punches, step or slip outside, as you block and strike. Execute at close range, or by charging 45° forward. Block the forearm, or elbow at TW-11. Strike the ribs at LV-13, or both GB-24 and LV-14. Pivot your shoulders and hips for power.

2. Block and Strike

A. Two-Hand Grab Parry
B. Pull forward and down
C. R Descending Knife Hand Strike

Step outside. Parry and grab opponent's arm with both hands. Unbalance them by pulling their arm forward and down. Raise your right hand, as you push down with the left hand. Strike downward to the cervical spine, or back of the neck at GB-20 or BL-10.

3. Block and Kick

A. R Inside Parry
B. L Rising Block and R Shin Kick
C. L Front Thrust Kick (with heel)

Step inward as you execute two blocks and a Shin Kick, in one fluid motion. The double blocks deflect a left-right combination. If opponent steps back, execute a Front Thrust Kick to the belly. If they are close, execute a right Rising Elbow Strike, or Inside Elbow Strike.

4. Block and Kick

A. R Outside Grab Parry
B. R Roundhouse Kick (Ball Foot)
C. L Inside Axe Kick (Back Heel)

Shift your weight to the back leg, as you parry and grab. Pull off-balance as you kick the testicles, or groin at LV-12 and SP-12. This bends opponent over for an Axe Kick to the spine at GV-15 or GV-12. If they don't bend, kick your left heel inward to the knee or spine.

5. Block and Hold

Attacker delivers a lead straight strike. Without stepping, lean back, parry with your R hand, and grip their wrist (A–B). Pull their wrist toward your right, twist their arm until their elbow points up, and plant your wrist slightly above the elbow at TW-11 (C). Step forcefully across to your right, pulling the elbow straight as you lock it. Drive downward at TW-11 with your wrist, as you lift attacker's wrist (D). Force a fall and pin.

Important Points

You must rotate attacker's arm, until their elbow points up. Your R hand twists attacker's wrist, by gripping their wrist and hand. Your L wrist drives up, over, and down (at the elbow), as you pull their wrist in the opposite direction. Begin pushing attacker's elbow at the *side of the joint,* and finish *above the back of the joint.* This rotates and locks attacker's elbow, even if their elbow is bent or facing sideways.

Direction of Force (lateral)

Push inward, and step forward and across, as you enter the arm bar. This allows you to stay in contact with the arm longer and increases your chances of grabbing the wrist. Even if you fail to secure a strong grip (attacker retracts), you can still trap the wrist by hooking with your R hand. In contrast, grabbing and pulling (180° pivot) is usually only effective against slow, lunging attacks. Stomp as you step across, for power.

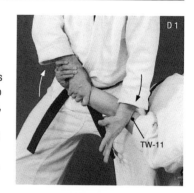

6. Block and Throw

Step inside a straight or inside circular strike. Block outward with your L hand and grip attacker's wrist (A–B). Twist their arm as you circle it downward to your right, passing it to your R hand. Wrap your L arm around their back (C). Step forward to your right with your L foot, pivot 180°, and pull attacker onto your hips. Lock their elbow across your chest, as your L hand gouges their ribs (D). Pull attacker over your hips (E).

Important Points

This is a devastating throw. To practice safely and prevent injuries, you must unlock the elbow and use the proper breakfall. As you step inward and across, plant your hips on attacker's thigh. When throwing, there are two common methods of generating lift: 1) raise your hips with both feet planted; or 2) swing your L leg up and back, which elevates your hip and propels attacker upward (E).

In Hapkido, kicks are countered using a blend of counterstrikes, holds, and throws. Technique selection and sequence is entirely up to the user. Regardless of how you attempt to counter a kick, you must first commit one of the following actions: block and counterstrike, block and apply a hold, or block and apply a throw (block means to block or avoid). Any of these three initial responses can be followed by additional strikes, holds, or throws, in any order you wish, as circumstances dictate. Because modern kicks can be delivered

DEFENSE AGAINST KICKS

with great speed and power, it is very important to learn proper footwork that allows you to avoid or engage a kick without getting injured. You can often avoid kicks by simply stepping closer (too close to be kicked), or stepping further away (out of range). The following pages show six typical techniques, organized based on the initial defensive response employed: strike, kick, hold, or throw. The author's 1136-page Hapkido book contains 60 defenses against kicks, and a detailed presentation of basic principles.

1. *Block and Strike*

A. R Inside Knife Hand Block
B. R Outside Knife Hand Strike
C. L Vertical Straight Punch

Step inside with your lead foot as you deflect the kick with a Knife Hand Block to the inner shin at SP-6. Do not hit into the top of the leg (opposing the kick), or you may break your hand. Follow with a R-L combo to the temple at M-HN-9, and solar plexus at CO-15.

2. *Block and Strike*

A. L Inside Hook Block (lift leg)
B. R Inside Elbow Strike
C. R Back Fist Strike

Step 45° forward to the outside as you block and lift. Hit down to the knee, or the nerve along the thigh (GB-30, 31, or 32). Follow with a Back Fist Strike to the back of the head (GB-20), or side of the jaw (TW-17). If the head is too far, hit the kidney (GB-25) or spine.

3. *Block and Kick*

A. Back step, X Block, grab ankle
B. Pull back, R Rising Front Kick
C. R Low Side Kick

Step back as you block and grab the ankle with both hands. Pull the leg up and back to unbalance, as you kick to either the back of the knee (BL-54), thigh (BL-51), or testicles. Without putting your foot down, kick the inner side of the knee to topple attacker.

4. *Block and Kick*

A. Two-Hand Wrap Block
B. R Rising Knee Strike
C. R Roundhouse Kick

Step forward, past attacker's heel. Your lead arm blocks as your rear arm wraps under the leg. Hold attacker's leg as you drive your knee up into their leg. Without putting your foot down, deliver a Roundhouse Kick to the left kneecap (support leg), groin, or head.

5. Block and Hold

Step forward and outside a Side Kick or Spin Kick. Block with the right or both forearms (A–B). As attacker plants their foot, grab their R hand with your L hand (C), then your R hand. Plant your thumbs on the back of the hand, between the 5th and 4th, and 3rd and 2nd knuckles (pressure points). Step back with your L foot. Pull attacker toward you, as you twist their hand outward and down to lock the wrist and force a fall (D–E).

Important Points

The specific block you use, depends on the height and type of kick you are defending against. Their are many possibilities. Generally, it is quicker to block with your right and grab with your left. Try to grab attacker's hand as it swings forward, or pauses in an extended position. Do this as they plant their foot, in the split-second pause before they begin their next motion. Twist the wrist in a tight circular motion to lock it.

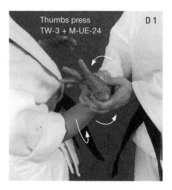
Thumbs press
TW-3 + M-UE-24   D 1

A

B

C

D

E

6. Block and Throw

Step inside a Front or Roundhouse Kick. Block inward with your lead forearm, as your rear arm wraps under the ankle (A). Lift attacker's leg as you cross-step inward, keeping your R hand held high to guard against strikes (B). Grab their shoulder with your R hand, driving your elbow into the face or throat. Place your R leg behind their support-leg. Reap the leg upward as you drive the upper body downward. A Back Fall is the proper fall.

Important Points

You must execute this throw quickly to avoid being punched in the face as you enter. As you step in (B), keep your hand high and in front, to protect your head. Try to use distracting strikes to set up the throw, linking them to grabs or unbalancing shoves. For example, hit and grab the shoulder as you drive your elbow into the face (C1). You can also drive your Palm Heel up into the chin or nose, pushing the head back.

C 1

A

A

B

C

D

All forms of holds possess specific limitations. To counter a hold, you must

capitalize on these inherent weaknesses and exploit them to your advantage.

In Hapkido, there are four basic methods of defense against holds: escape,

strike-and-escape, counterhold, and throw. Any of these basic methods can be

linked to additional strikes, holds, or throws, as circumstances dictate.

Generally, you should respond first with a simple escape, or a counterhold to

control your opponent. If this is ineffective, progress to more forceful strikes

DEFENSE AGAINST HOLDS

or throws. Since striking or throwing constitutes a greater use of force, this

will escalate the situation, forcing your opponent to respond similarly.

Whether you respond gently or with force is a matter of choice, mostly

determined by the situation and common sense. The following pages show

20 typical techniques. They have been organized based on the type of attack,

which is how the art of Hapkido is structured and taught. The author's

1136-page Hapkido book includes over 160 typical defenses against holds.

BASIC LEADING MOTIONS

When executing counters against wrist holds, it is often important to make an initial deceptive movement. Generally, this means moving your hand or faking in the opposite direction you intend to move. This causes your opponent to react in a manner which leads them into your countertechnique. The basic principles of *leading* are covered in detail in the author's 1136-page book.

The leading motions shown below and on the next page are used to enter many of the escapes and counterholds shown later in this chapter. Many other possibilities exist and are far too numerous and varied to show.

In fact, many leading motions often involve a combination of several contradictory movements. The precise motions you choose to make will often depend on your opponent's reactions. For example, if you pull your hand to your hip, hoping your opponent will pull back to assist your entry—and they do not—merely continue into another hold, based on your initial motion.

Long vs. Short Movements

Do not become overly concerned with long movements vs. short movements. Although there is currently a great deal of debate regarding the relative merits of each, both have their place and purpose. Generally,

motions should be selected to suit the holds that are being applied, and the unique dynamics of a confrontation. If you try to respond according to some narrowly defined concept of right and wrong, you are merely creating your own limitations, and sowing the seeds of your own failure. It is easy to say (and to believe) that short, quick, and simple is always best. In many situations, it certainly is. However, against highly skilled or much stronger opponents, more aggressive and pronounced movement is often needed in order to create opportunity for your counters. Against multiple attackers, pronounced leading and footwork is often used to make targeting difficult and generate confusion.

1. Inward Lead

2. Outward Lead

Typical Examples

The following basic leading motions are used to enter many of the counterholds used against wrist grabs. These same principles are also applied against a variety of other simple holds, including clothing grabs and body grabs. The actual motions may be quite different, although the principle is the same.

1. Inward Lead

This is used when you wish to turn an opponent's wrist inward, entering counterholds such as a Bent-Arm Wrist Lock, Straight-Arm Wrist Lock, or arm bar. Spread your fingers in a Live-Hand (A). Make a brief motion inward (B), then circle your hand outward and up (C).

2. Outward Lead

This is used to turn an opponent's wrist outward, entering counterholds such as an Outward Wrist Lock, Scoop Wrist Lock, or Outside Hip Throw. Spread your fingers in a Live-Hand (A). Make a brief motion outward (B), then circle your hand inward and up (C).

3. Backward Lead

This is used when you wish to step inward or pass under an attacker's arm, applying wrist escapes or holds such as an Elevated Wrist Lock, Hammer Lock, or Twisting Arm Lock. Form a Live-Hand (A). Pull your hand toward your hip (B). Push forward and step inward, as the opponent resists or pulls back (C).

4. Forward Lead

This is used when you wish to straighten the attacker's arm, entering counterholds such as a Forearm Arm Bar or Extended-Arm Arm Bar. It can also be used to break the elbow as shown in the example. As the opponent grabs your wrist or hand (A), push your hand toward their hip (B), then pull back toward your body as the opponent resists or pushes back (C).

Two-Hand Leads

The same leading motions used against single wrist grabs can also be applied when both wrists are held. Typical examples are covered in the author's 1136-page book, under *Defense Against Grab to Both Wrists*.

3. Backward Lead

4. Forward Lead

BASIC WRIST ESCAPES

Wrist escapes are used to free your hand(s) from simple holds to one or both wrists. These escapes are among the first defensive hand techniques to be learned, and constitute one of the most basic and important forms of self-defense. If you can do nothing else, you must be able to remove yourself from danger and maintain control of your own body. This is fundamental to launching any counter. Mastering basic escapes is also essential because these same movements are also used when entering many joint locks and holds. The examples on the following pages show escapes from a grab to the opposite wrist. Cross-hand escapes are usually similar.

When executing any wrist escape, you must focus on changing the relationship between your wrist and the attacker's hand. This involves leverage principles and physics, not strength, or wildly swinging your hand to and fro. In most escapes, your arm pivots on an imaginary axis projecting through your wrist.

Live-Hand Use

Historically, Hapkido wrist escapes have always made use of Live-Hand formations. This increases the efficiency of your escape by expanding the forearm, increasing Ki-flow, and tensing your arm muscles in a manner permitting greater arm strength. If your technique is efficient, you don't need a Live-Hand to make it work. However, against a much larger, stronger opponent, it may provide the edge you need to make your escape. Against a powerful grip, you may also need to use initial strikes to assist an escape.

Leading

Always use *leading* to set up the escape. Generally, this means moving your hand or faking in the opposite direction you intend to move. Although there is much debate about long-traditional leading vs. short-modern leading, both have their purposes. It is the circumstances that are most important. Use short, abrupt leading for speed, surprise, and to prevent an attacker from adjusting.

1. Rising Wrist Escape (circular twisting path)

2. Outside Wrist Escape

Use long leading to create movement. This is useful against clumsy attackers, or when short leading is ineffective. When one escape is not working, make a transition to another. The larger book shows 14 basic techniques.

1. Rising Wrist Escape (circular twist)

Spread your fingers in a Live-Hand and pull down (A). Quickly reverse direction, bringing your hand upward in a circular motion, with your palm facing you (B). An attacker's grip is much weaker in this position. Twist your hand and pull back, as you drive your elbow up toward the attacker's midline (C). Twist your forearm as you escape, driving the thin edge of your wrist through their thumb and fingers.

2. Outside Wrist Escape

Spread your fingers in a Live-Hand (A). Step forward to the attacker's outside. Turn your hand so your inner wrist is facing the opening between the attacker's thumb and fingers (B). Pull your hand back and drive your elbow toward the attacker's forearm, levering against the web of the thumb (C). The entire motion follows a horizontal path. Rotate your hips and shoulders to generate power.

3. Inside Wrist Escape

Spread your fingers in a Live-Hand (A). Step forward to the attacker's inside, driving your free elbow or shoulder into the chest or head (strike can be omitted). Turn your palm up and drive your hand away from the attacker (B). Keep your elbow tight to your side as you lever free (C). The entire motion follows a horizontal circular path. For power, rotate your hips and shoulders as you apply the escape.

4. Descending Wrist Escape

Spread your fingers in a Live-Hand formation; make a short rising motion. Quickly reverse direction and lever your wrist toward the web of the thumb (A), as you step forward (B). Bring your elbow up, forward, and down into the attacker's forearm, as you twist your wrist (C). The elbow follows a vertical circular path, with your wrist acting as a fulcrum. For power, rotate your shoulders and sink your hips.

3. Inside Wrist Escape

4. Descending Wrist Escape

1. Opposite-Wrist Grab

Form a Live-Hand (A). Trap attacker's hand on your wrist, with your L hand. Pull back and lead inward (fake) (B). Push forward and circle your R hand outward and over, grabbing their wrist in the "V" between your thumb and index finger (C). Lock the wrist toward the forearm, as you twist their hand forward. Pull down and back at their wrist with your other hand (use upper-body weight). Drop to one knee, pin (D–E).

Important Points

There are more than 19 variations in methods of gripping (shown in the author's larger book). Regardless of how you grip, keep attacker's held-hand pointing toward the vertical midline of their body. Lock their wrist sideways and forward as you twist their hand, focusing force at SI-5. Ideally, attacker's elbow and wrist are bent about 90°. Even if their arm is partially extended, the hold still works reasonably well.

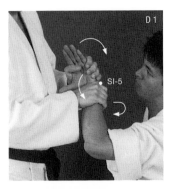

2. Cross-Wrist Grab

Lead outward (fake). Circle your hand inward, up, and over, gripping attacker's wrist overhand, as your L hand grips underhand. Step in with your R foot, as you twist-pull attacker's arm toward you to unbalance them (B). Step behind their R leg with your L foot, bend low, and pull them onto your shoulders (C). Pull their wrist down (locks elbow), lift their inner knee with your L hand, and rise upward, throwing them across your shoulders (E).

Important Points

When entering, attacker's weight must be moving forward, as you twist their arm to position their elbow for the arm bar. Initial strikes to stun or lower their head will help set up the throw. Once the elbow is locked on your shoulder (D), the technique is strong. If needed, break the elbow by pulling their leg down, as you pull their wrist. When throwing, coordinate three actions: pull the wrist across your waist, lift the inner knee, and rise.

3. Double Grab to One Wrist

Form a Live-Hand (A). Step back, pull down (B), lead outward. Step forward between attacker's legs as you circle your hand inward and over their wrist (C). This locks attacker's R wrist with their arms tangled. You can also reverse your motion to lock their other wrist (D1). Throw by driving the edge of your hand (or palm) toward attacker's face, as you grip behind their knee (middle finger at BL-54) and pull (D–E).

Important Points

This throw is applied in one quick, fluid motion, before an attacker can release their grips or recover their balance. Initial leading is crucial, in order to overcome the superior strength of your opponent's two-hand grip. Make sure you step deep between their legs, in a Back Stance, to protect your groin from being kicked as they fall. You must grab their knee *before* pushing, or they can step backward to recover their balance.

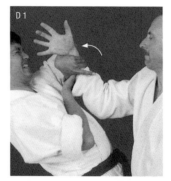

4. Grab to Both Wrists

Form Live-Hands (A). Step toward the attacker's R foot with your R foot. Lead your R hand inward so your L hand can grab their cross-wrist (B). Step closer with your L foot and pivot 180°. As you enter, lift and lock their elbow with your upper arm, and lever your R hand free (C). Keep pulling as you wrap both arms, locking the elbows (D). Pull the arms down, bend forward, raise your hips, and throw over your shoulder (E).

Important Points

Basically, you will leverage your hand free using an *Outside Wrist Escape,* as you grab the other wrist. When entering, you must pull forcefully, to straighten opponent's arms and unbalance them forward. Plant your shoulder in the armpits, and your hip against their right inner thigh (D). Exercise caution, since an opponent's elbows and shoulder can easily dislocate. A skilled opponent will land using a Side Fall or a Bridge Fall.

5. Clothing Grab

Attacker grabs your sleeve at the elbow. Grip their elbow with your L hand, pressing your thumb into PC-3 or HT-3 (A). Form a Live-Hand and clamp your elbow closed, trapping their hand. Step 45° forward with the R foot and lift the elbow (B). Step under the arm with your L foot. Pivot 180° as you lock the shoulder (C). Plant your R hand in the elbow (D). Drive your Knife Hand down, as you lift your elbow (and trapped wrist). Force a fall (E).

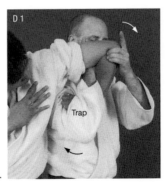

Trap

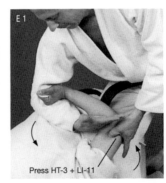

Press HT-3 + LI-11

6. Chest Push

Step back continuously as you absorb attacker's push, trap their hand on your chest (A–B), pull their arm straight, and twist their hand till the little finger faces up. Grip with two hands. Lock the wrist: pull inward at the wrist with your little fingers, as you lever their hand forward (C). Execute a Front Kick to the chin, as you wrap your leg over their arm (D–E) to lock the elbow. Bend and twist their hand, to lock the wrist and shoulder (F).

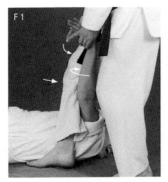

SI-5

7. Grab From Behind (wrists)

Both wrists are pulled up and back (A). Bend and twist your arms behind your back. Thrust your Live Hands to the right as you pivot (B); repeat to the left (C). Pivot right and redirect your L arm over your head, passing outside as you grab both wrists (D). Cross attacker's arms; lock their L elbow at TW-11, with their R forearm (E). Drive your R hand down, pull your L hand up (F). Pull toward their left front-corner, drop to one knee, and pin.

Important Points

The twisting-arm-swings and three body pivots create space and redirect opponent's energy so you can overcome their superior strength and enter the hold. Twisting your wrists during steps B–D weakens attacker's grips, and often causes them to release your wrists. When grabbing both wrists, use overhand grips (D, E1). If you grip incorrectly, it will be difficult to apply the subsequent arm lock.

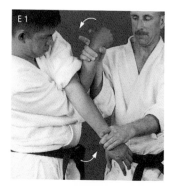

8. Grab From Behind (sleeves)

Attacker grips both sleeves at the elbow (A). Form Live Hands. Step back with the L foot (B). Step behind their legs with the R foot, plant your shoulder on the chest. Grip the backs of both knees, pressing your fingers into BL-54 (C). Pull forward and scoop the legs up, as you push their torso back with your shoulder. Lift high and drop attacker on their head or back (D); or drop them on your knee and deliver a Descending Elbow Strike (D1).

Important Points

Before lifting, unbalance attacker backward by using your upper body to push, and your hands to pull. This shifts their body weight off their legs, making it easier to lift them. Even if you are unable to lift the legs, this *push-pull* action will cause a fall in most cases. Pulling at the knees, also prevents attacker from stepping back to recover their balance. When scooping, pull tight to your body and lift with your legs (not your back).

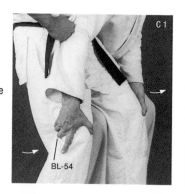

9. Bear-Hug From Front

Attacker hugs, pinning your arms (A). Lift your R foot, form Thumb Hands (B). Stomp their instep or toes, gouge both thumbs into the hip joint at SP-12 (C), or ribs at GB-25. This loosens the hug, creates maneuvering space, and frees your lower arms. Lower your body, reach around the shoulders, plant both hands on the face (thumbs press nerves under jaw, fingers gouge eyes and cheek). Push up, back, and down. Throw (D–E).

Important Points

You must first create space, otherwise you will never be able to grip the head. The acupoints you are able to reach (C) depend upon: how tightly you are held, how much lower-arm movement is possible, and the relative sizes of your bodies. Any sensitive point you can reach will suffice. You can also pinch a small amount of skin at the front of the thigh; or at the side of the waist, just above the crest of the iliac bone.

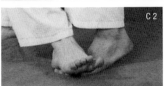
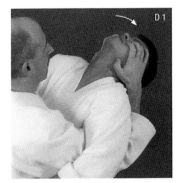

10. Bear-Hug From Behind

Attacker hugs, pinning your arms. Rise on your toes, pull your hips forward, and lift your hands to your waist (A). Thrust both Spear Hands into the groin at SP-12 and LV-12 (B). Drop your hips and thrust your Live-Hands up, to break the hold (C). Grip attacker's cross-wrist and pull them into a Back Elbow Strike to the ribs (D). Wrap their arm and seat your hips on their thigh (E). Bend forward, raise your hips, and pull over your shoulder (F).

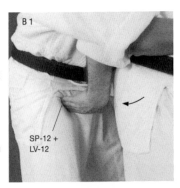

SP-12 + LV-12

11. Head Hold (hair pull)

Attacker grabs your hair (A). Trap their hand on your head, with both hands (B): L fingers grip edge of palm, L thumb presses base joint of thumb, R hand grips wrist in "V" between thumb and index finger. Step across and twist attacker's hand until their elbow points up. Lock the wrist (C). Lock the elbow by driving your inner elbow down into the joint, as you lift the wrist (D). Pin from a kneeling or standing posture (E).

Important Points

Locking attacker's wrist as you apply the arm bar is useful, since this helps turn their elbow, lower their shoulder, and generate additional pain. As you lock the elbow, push on attacker's knuckles to lock their wrist (D1). If attacker bends their elbow, shift to a Bent-Arm Wrist Lock (see technique 1). The basic entry shown below can also be used to apply a variety of other wrist locks, arm bars, and shoulder locks.

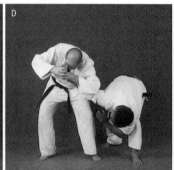

12. Head Hold (full nelson)

Full Nelson (A). Poke the eyes with a Five-Fingertip Hand, as you lift your leg (B). Stomp the toes. Press nerves at the back of the hand, with an Index Finger Fist. As the hold loosens, peel back one or two fingers with your other hand (C). Lock the finger back, step outside, pivot 180° (D). Step back, force attacker to their belly (E). Many other finger locks are possible, based on which hand you grab with, and which fingers are held.

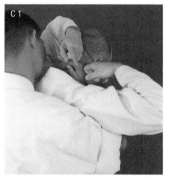
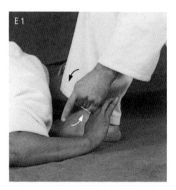

The objective of most choke holds is to force submission, cause loss of consciousness, or effect death. In self-defense situations, forcing submission is rarely the objective of your attacker. Consequently, any choke must be considered a serious threat, even if it appears incompetent. A choke that is loose and ineffectual could easily become life threatening in the span of a moment. A simple grip shift, or an adjustment in an attacker's technique, can make all the difference. Once a strong choke is applied to the carotid artery,

DEFENSE AGAINST CHOKES

you will pass-out in 10–15 seconds. Chokes to the front of the neck are even more serious, since collapse of the trachea can block the air supply, resulting in death. In Hapkido, defenses against chokes are commonly organized based on the type of attack. Categories include front choke, front naked choke, side choke, and rear naked choke. Some typical examples are shown on the following pages. The author's 1136-page Hapkido book contains 26 choke defenses, and a comprehensive discussion of important defensive principles.

1. Against Front Choke

Attacker chokes with two hands (A). Step away, grip their cross-hand with one hand, poke the throat using any Spear Hand (B). Hit CO-22, or ST-9 and ST-10. As the choke releases, twist their hand inward and hit the inner elbow with your L Ridge Hand (bends wrist and elbow). Lock their wrist by rotating their hand toward their body midline. Pull the wrist down and back with your L hand (C–D), or shift to a one-hand hold (C2).

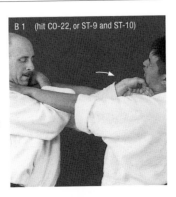

B 1   (hit CO-22, or ST-9 and ST-10)

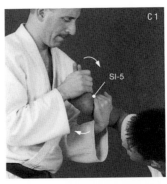

C 1

SI-5

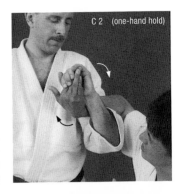

C 2   (one-hand hold)

A

B

C

D

2. Against Front Naked Choke

Attacker applies a Front Naked Choke (A). Relieve pressure by pulling down on their arm with your L hand. The following strikes can be used singly or combined: Hook Punch to head (B), Spear Hand to throat at CO-22 (C), Rising Thumb Fist to testicles (D). As the choke loosens, drop your L hand down and pull the ankle, as you thrust a R Spear Hand into the groin at SP-12 and LV-12 (E), forcing a fall (F). Step C can also be used to force a fall.

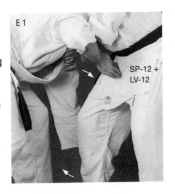

E 1

SP-12 + LV-12

A

B

C   (spear throat)

D   (Rising Thumb Fist)

E   (spear groin)

F

3. Against Side Choke

Attacker applies a Side Naked Choke (A). Relieve pressure by pulling their arm down with your L hand, as you deliver a Hook Punch to the jaw at TW-17, or the lower-rear skull at GB-20 (B). Lift the underside of their chin backward with your L palm, as you scoop their knee forward, gouging BL-54. Throw backward (C–E). If attacker maintains their head-hold during D, lift high and slam, dropping on top of them (F–G).

Important Points

The initial punch loosens or releases the choke, to set up the throw. You can also throw without striking. When pushing the head back, you can also gouge your fingertips into the eyes, cheek, or throat; or reach behind the neck to the far shoulder and pull ST-11. The slam option (F–G) is a high-impact fall and usually knocks the air out of the lungs, or injures the spine. Pushing the head down as you drop, smashes the skull into the ground.

G (Leg-Lift Slam Throw)

A

B (Hook Punch to jaw)

C

D

E

4. Against Rear Naked Choke

Attacker applies a Rear Naked Choke (A). Drop your chin to protect the throat. Reduce pressure by pulling their arm down with both hands, as you step back with the R foot, past their leg (B). Pull their arm down as you drop to one knee, blocking their foot with your inner knee (C). This keeps attacker from stepping around to counter. Bend deeply forward, pulling them over your shoulder (D–E). You can also throw while standing (D1).

Important Points

Although standing throws are an option, this throw is most powerful when dropping. This allows you to use your entire body weight to assist the throw. Make sure you trap attacker's leg as you drop, planting your buttocks on their lower leg. The bodies are locked tight together as you throw. Most errors result from excess space. As you bend forcefully forward, drive your head toward your L leg (E).

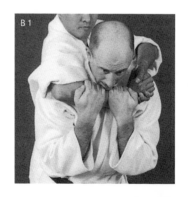
B 1

D 1 (standing throw)

A

B

C

D (side view)

E (side view)

In Hapkido, joint lock holds are an important form of self-defense, used to control and restrain an opponent's movement. However, it is also possible that these same techniques may be used against you. Proficiency in applying joint lock holds in combat situations takes years to master. Consequently, most joint lock attacks directed at you are likely to come from skilled opponents. Their level of skill determines the degree of danger they pose. Since most joint locks can cause serious damage—broken bones or torn muscles, tendons, and

DEFENSE AGAINST JOINT LOCKS

ligaments—your first concern is always to nullify the hold and protect your joints. Defenses Against Joint Locks are advanced techniques learned at the black belt level, although there is no reason they cannot be learned sooner. However, before learning these techniques, you must first learn how to apply all the holds you will be defending against. Typical defenses are shown on the following pages. The author's 1136-page Hapkido book contains 40 typical defenses, and a comprehensive discussion of important defensive principles.

1. Against Bent-Arm Wrist Lock
Use Bent-Arm Wrist Lock

As wrist lock is applied (A), reach across with your free L hand and grab the hand holding your wrist (B): fingers grip edge of palm, thumb presses LI-4 in web of thumb. Twist attacker's hand inward, as you rotate your R elbow over their forearm. Their wrist and elbow are bent about 90° (C). Lock the wrist by twisting their hand forward, as you push your R arm down into their forearm (D).

Important Points

In this counter, you will apply the same hold to your attacker, that they apply to you. As you reach across, press your L arm down into their arms (B1). This limits their wrist and arm movements, preventing them from fully applying the wrist lock. As you apply the counter, use your R arm to push down and inward, keeping their wrist and arm close to your body (D). Maneuver your upper body over the hold, to assist leverage.

2. Against Forearm Arm Bar
Use Passing Armpit Arm Bar

Twist attacker's fingers, lock their joints, and push up, as you pivot left (A–B). Pull your L hand free. Twist their hand with both hands, step under the arm with your R foot, pivot 180° (C). Twist their hand till the elbow points up. Place your arm over the elbow (D). Push down to lock it, as you lift the wrist. Bend and twist the wrist to lock it. Step 45° forward with your R foot, drop to your L knee, pin (E).

3. Against Elbow Arm Bar

Use Turning Elbow Strike + Outer Reap
As attacker enters an arm bar (A): pivot 180°, bend your arm behind your back (B), and deliver an Outside Elbow Strike to the base of the skull at GB-20, BL-10, GV-15, or GV-16 (C). Sweep your arm past their head, and wrap their neck. Plant your inner elbow on their throat, and lift their chin with your elbow (D). Throw by pulling the head down as you sweep your leg back into the calf (E).

Important Points
When clamping attacker's neck, try to apply a choke, using your tensed biceps, lower arm muscles, and edge of your forearm. You will be pressing to both sides of their neck at the carotid artery (ST-9 and ST-10). Rather than choking, you can also hit into the throat with your Inner Elbow or Inner Forearm, as you reap their leg. Try to grab their wrist and pull their arm as you throw. Drive your upper body forward and down for power.

 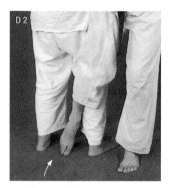

4. Against Bent-Wrist Hammer

Use Drop Head Hip Throw
Attacker locks your arm behind you (A). Before the hold is tight: step back with your R foot, turn toward attacker, and swing your free arm past their head (B). Wrap attacker's neck with your arm (C). Pull their head down as you drop to one knee, blocking their foot with your inner knee (D). This keeps them from stepping around to counter. Bend deeply forward, pulling attacker over your hip (E).

Important Points
You must start before the Hammer Lock is tight. Otherwise, attacker can easily prevent you from turning. As you reach back to wrap their neck, you can also hit their head with an Outside Elbow Strike. Don't hit too hard or you will knock their head out of reach. As you execute your throw, attacker will usually release their arm hold. If they don't let go, or you feel your shoulder being locked, flip over and land on top of them as they fall.

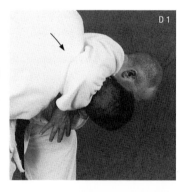

Executing any throw requires four basic actions: secure a grip, unbalance the opponent, position the body, and execute the throw. These actions must be well timed for a throw to be successful. Naturally, any defense against a throw must attempt to prevent one or more of these actions from occurring. If you can do this, you will weaken your opponent's technique, causing the throw to fail. When defending against throws, there are four basic moments when a defensive counter can be launched: as the attacker tries to grab; at the moment

DEFENSE AGAINST THROWS

grips are secured; during the throw; and after the throw. Before learning these techniques, you should first learn how to apply all the throws you will be defending against. This allows you to understand their specific weaknesses. You should also be skilled in executing the eight forms of breakfalls covered earlier in this book. Typical defenses against throws are shown on the following pages. The author's 1136-page Hapkido book contains 40 common defenses, and a comprehensive discussion of important defensive principles.

1. Against Shoulder or Hip Throw
Use Descending Arch Kick

Attacker grips your sleeve and lapel (A). As they pull you forward and step in and pivot, lower your center of gravity. Push their R arm down (grip at the elbow), as you pull their L arm toward you (B). Lift either leg and thrust the inner edge of your foot down into the rear-inner knee, or back of the knee at BL-54 (C–D). This collapses their leg, forcing a Front Fall and smashing the kneecap.

Important Points

Pushing and pulling attacker's arms (B), usually prevents them from pivoting inward. Do not pick up your leg, unless you arrest their motion. Otherwise, you can be easily unbalanced, since you will be standing on one leg. Driving your foot into their knee, also prevents them from pivoting their body to complete the throw. Without this hip-turn and hip-lift, it is very difficult to generate sufficient force to initiate a hip or shoulder throw.

2. Against Hip Throw
Use Outer Reap Throw

Attacker pulls your R arm and steps in to execute a hip throw. As they step across and pivot (A), step across with your R foot, pivot 180°, and plant your R leg behind their leg. Wrap their neck, pull their arm to your waist. Unbalance them backward (B). Throw by pulling their head forward and down, as you sweep your R leg back into their leg (C). Continue to hold their arm. Strike (D).

Important Points

This counter requires anticipation, speed, and timing. You must begin your pivot in unison with attacker's pivot, by stepping across, *before* they plant their R foot. Once they plant their foot and hips, you will no longer have the space or time to step. Also, attacker's balance is most vulnerable during their step, since they are supported on one leg. You can reap any part of the leg (ankle, calf, thigh), depending on your position.

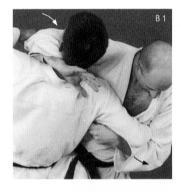

3. Against Inner Reap

Use Corner Throw

Attacker reaps your leg toward their body, to force a Back Fall (A–B). Drop to your back, in front of attacker, kicking your R instep up into the back of their knee or thigh. As you drop, grip their sleeves or lapels and pull them over your L shoulder, as you lift their leg with your R instep (C–D). Attacker will land on their side or back. Roll on top of them, or return to a standing position.

Important Points

This counter can be applied much later in attacker's entry, even after your balance has been broken, or as you are thrown backward. Pull hard and drop *under* opponent. You can also counter by using a *Circle Throw* (plant foot in groin, lift, pull over head, C2), or by using a *Side Drop Throw* (lift knee, pull laterally). All of these counters use similar entries, although you will be using your legs and arms differently (see *Throws* chapter).

C 2 (Circle Throw option)

A

B

C (side view)

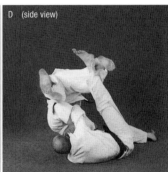

D (side view)

4. Against Push-Pull Throw

Use Parry, Trap, Rear Push Throw

Attacker pulls your belt, as they push your chin with their R hand (A). Turn your torso sideways and step back with your R foot to stabilize balance (B). Parry their high-arm inward and down with your L arm, in a circular motion. Trap their arm against your body, place your knee behind their knee (C). Thrust your elbow back into their throat, as you lift your knee slightly, forcing a Back Fall (D–E).

Important Points

Attacker's throw will only work if they can drive your head and hips in opposing directions. Turning your body, or deflecting one of attacker's hands, will negate their leverage. As you enter, lower your body for stability. The elbow strike can be gentle or forceful. Rotate your upper body for power (E). This throw can also be executed by sweeping your extended arm backward into the throat or base of the nose.

A

B

C

D (Rear Push Throw)

E

Not all confrontations can be resolved from a standing position. You may be forced to the ground, or you may already be there. Consequently, your ability to defend from the ground is as important as your ability to fight while standing. Today, this reality is widely acknowledged in many styles. Many martial arts systems which did not originally include ground techniques are currently incorporating them into their repertories. In Hapkido, ground defenses have existed since its origin. Techniques are executed from kneeling,

GROUND DEFENSES

sitting, or reclining positions against opponents operating from any position, including airborne, standing, kneeling, sitting, or reclining. As with standing techniques, specific methods of locomotion are used to facilitate execution of offensive or defensive techniques, or to remove oneself from the area of confrontation. Typical ground defenses are shown on the following pages. The author's 1136-page Hapkido book contains 54 common ground defenses, and a comprehensive presentation of Hapkido ground fighting principles.

1. Seated Defense

Standing attacker grabs your wrist (A). Grip the back of the opposite ankle with your R hand. At the same time, leverage your L wrist free, as you reach across and press your L forearm into nerves on the inner shin or lower knee (B). Press the shin as you pull the ankle toward you. This generates pain, forcing a Back Fall (C). Wrap the ankle (Achilles Ankle Lock), lift, turn over, and transition to a Single-Leg Crab Lock (D–E).

Important Points

Although this example shows a defense against a wrist grab, it can be used in a variety of situations. Your R hand keeps attacker from pulling their leg away, as your L forearm presses nerves on their lower leg. Potential nerve targets exist at different heights. Common pressure points from low to high are at SP-6, LV-6, SP-8, and SP-9. You can also reverse the roles of your hands (grip with L hand, press L shin with R hand).

2. Seated Defense

Attacker is standing in front, choking you or grabbing your lapel (A). Grip their lapel with one hand; grip their sleeve under the elbow, with your other hand (B). If sleeveless, grip bare elbows. Pull attacker toward you. Kick your foot into their groin, belly (C1), solar plexus, or hip joint (C2). Roll backward and pull them over your head, as you extend your leg to lift (D). You can also throw by planting your shins against their shins (C3).

3. Reclining Defense

Attacker advances from the front. From a Seated Guard (L foot lead), execute two Front Blade Kicks to the groin (R first, then L) (A–B). Snap your R heel outward, executing a Circular Inner-Heel Kick to the kneecap or inner knee (C). Hook your R heel inward, executing an Inside Hook Kick to the outer knee (D–E). Hook the ankle with your R leg. Thrust your L Spear Foot into the groin at SP-12 and LV-12, forcing a fall (F–G).

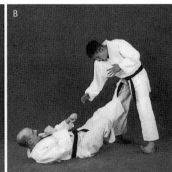

4. Reclining Defense

Attacker straddles your torso and chokes. Press CO-22 with a Spear Hand, as you grab their opposite wrist with your L hand (A). Twist their hand outward to lock the wrist (thumb presses TW-3, fingers pull edge of palm). Grip their fingers with your R hand (thumb down) and twist to assist the wrist lock. Roll sideways and arch as attacker falls sideways (C). Apply a Tiger Mouth Choke. Pull back on their wrist, locking the elbow on your knee (D).

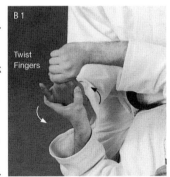
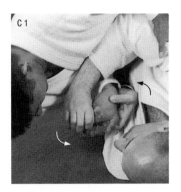
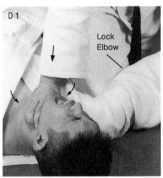

When defending against strikes, holds, and throws, Hapkido counterattacks may also be initiated by using just one hand—or sometimes no hands. This type of counter may be useful when: one or both arms are damaged or restrained; one hand is holding a weapon; one hand is holding or protecting something, such as an infant; you are countering simultaneous attacks from multiple opponents; or you are physically handicapped and do not possess the use of an arm. The ability to counter with one arm is the mark of any highly

DEFENSE USING ONE OR NO ARMS

skilled Hapkidoist. One-arm or no-arm defenses employ the same basic techniques and principles used in two-hand techniques. Naturally, you must understand the mechanics of basic joint locks and throws before applying their one-hand versions, otherwise you are likely to become quite frustrated. Typical techniques are shown on the following pages. The author's 1136-page Hapkido book contains more than 36 typical defenses applied using one or no arms. Most of these defenses are commonly learned at the black belt level.

1. One-Arm Defense

Attacker grabs your wrist. Form a Live-Hand (A). Step 45° forward with the R foot. Lead your hand outward (B). Step under the arm with the L foot, pivot 180° (C). Lead their arm behind their back, briefly lock their wrist and fingers (D1). Snake your arm around their arm. Plant your R hand in their elbow; trap their wrist in your elbow. Lock the shoulder by driving your Knife Hand down, as you lift your elbow (E). Pivot left and throw (F).

2. One-Arm Defense

Attacker steps forward and executes a R punch. Step 45° forward with your R foot, inside the blow (A). Block with your palm and grip their sleeve. Pull attacker off balance and blend with their force (B). Step behind your R foot with your L foot, pivot 180°. Pull their arm, as you plant your hips low, and seat your shoulder in their armpit (C). Pull down, raise your hips, bend forward, throw over your shoulder (D).

Important Points

This throw can be used against a Hook Punch, Straight Punch, or a descending strike. Footwork is very important, since you must blend with attacker's force, using your body-spin to generate the throw. Often you will need to pivot more than 180°, in order to properly position your hips. You can grip at a variety of points on the arm, including the wrist. As you throw, raise your elbow to provide lift.

3. No-Arms Defense

This hold is executed without using your arms or hands. Attacker grabs your lapel with their L hand (A). Step forward with your L foot as you bend low (B). Circle your head under their arm (C), as you step across with the R foot and pivot 180°. Their hand becomes trapped and twisted in your clothing (D). Continue to turn your body, locking the wrist, fingers, and arm outward. Lower you body and pull down to unbalance and throw (E).

Important Points

This counter requires strong clothing, such as a jacket or heavy shirt. It is unlikely to be effective if you are wearing a T-shirt, since the fabric stretches. If you can use one hand, pull your lapels down as you pivot. This traps attacker's hand tightly in your clothing, and will lock their joints sooner, when you turn. If the hold is too loose, pass under their arm a second time. If they bend their arm, shift to a shoulder lock.

4. No-Arms Defense

This hold is executed without using your arms or hands. Attacker grabs the center of your belt (A). It doesn't matter whether their palm faces up or down. Raise your R knee and plant it on top of attacker's inner elbow (B–C). Push straight down, using your body weight to drive their elbow into the ground (D). You can continue to kneel on their elbow, pinning their arm (very painful), or stand up and execute kicks (E).

Important Points

Anytime you raise one leg, your balance is vulnerable. Consequently, you must execute this hold very quickly, before attacker can pull you off-balance, or release their hold on your belt. Commit your entire body weight into the hold, pulling attacker toward their front or front-corner. Adjust the direction of your throw based on their foot placement. If you lose control of their arm during step D, immediately stand up and kick.

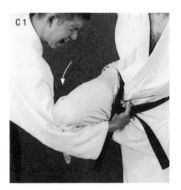

There are two fundamental platforms for launching techniques: attacking or counterattacking. In attacking, you will decide when to initiate an offensive action. In counterattacking, you will respond based upon your opponent's actions. All fighting is essentially a blending of these two basic modes. Although Hapkido is self-defense oriented, there are times when you must attack first. This is particularly true of encounters with multiple opponents. In Hapkido, attacks are classified according to the type of technique initially

ATTACKING TECHNIQUES

employed. There are three basic categories: offensive strikes, offensive holds, and offensive throws. Generally, these categories only exist for purposes of organizing and teaching basic skills. In reality, techniques are blended together as required by circumstances. For example, a strike attack might create opportunities for a joint lock or a throw. An attacking hold that meets strong resistance may require strikes to assist the technique. The following pages show five typical techniques. The author's 1136-page book contains hundreds.

1. Offensive Strike

From a relaxed stance (A), step forward with your L foot. Pull opponent's R elbow with your L hand (B), as you swing your R Ridge Hand into the upper lip at GV-26 (philtrum). You can also hit ST-9 and ST-10 on the neck , hitting both acupoints with one blow (C). Follow with additional strikes, holds, or throws as circumstances dictate. Exercise caution during practice when targeting ST acupoints.

2. Offensive Combo Strike

From a relaxed stance (A), step forward with your R foot. Pull opponent's R lapel with your L hand, as you execute a R Palm Heel Strike to the solar plexus at CO-15 (B). Retract your R arm, then execute a R Rising Elbow Strike to the underside of the chin (C). Pulling the opponent's lapel adds force to your strikes by pulling them into your blows. Drive upward with your legs and hips, during the elbow strike.

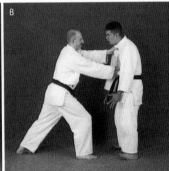

3. Offensive Hold

From a relaxed stance (A), step forward to your left, with your L foot. Grip opponent's R hand with both hands, placing your thumbs on the back of their hand (B). Step under their arm with your R foot, as you twist their hand and pivot 180° (C). Continue to twist (locks the arm and shoulder), as you whip their arm forward and down (D), to force a fall or dislocation. A skilled opponent will initiate a fall to save their arm (E).

Important Points

This hold locks opponent's wrist, arm, and shoulder by step C, usually causing serious injuries. It can be applied with opponent's arm either bent or straight. You can pass under their arm close to their body or farther away. When passing under opponent's arm, keep their hand twisted in front of your head, to prevent counters. As you exit, pull their arm forcefully forward, forcing them to step past you. You can also drop to one knee.

4. Offensive Throw

From a relaxed stance (A), step forward with your R foot. Grab opponent's R wrist with your L hand. Pull them toward you, as you execute a R Straight Punch to their solar plexus (B). Wrap their arm, plant your shoulder in their armpit, and lock their elbow with your wrist (C1). Step behind your R foot with your L foot and pivot 180°, planting your hips on their R thigh (C). Raise your hips and pull opponent over your shoulder (D).

Important Points

Apply the arm bar by pressing your wrist into TW-11. You can break opponent's elbow by hitting into the joint as you wrap their arm, or by locking the joint as they fall. Both bodies should be pressed tightly together, with your shoulder seated deeply in the armpit. As you pull opponent's arm down and lift with your hips, their shoulder will separate. During training, place their armpit against your outer shoulder to prevent damage.

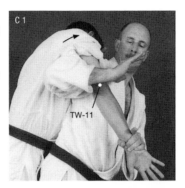

5. Offensive Throw

From a relaxed stance (A), step forward with your L foot (B). Without pausing, swing your R foot between opponent's legs and plant it behind their L knee or calf. Grip behind their R knee with your L hand, pressing your middle finger into BL-54. At the same time, lift their chin and push it backward with your R Palm Heel (C). As you push their chin, pull both knees toward you, forcing a Back Fall (D). Your R heel will reap the L leg.

Important Points

This throw produces a very jarring fall. Since both of opponent's legs are trapped, it is difficult for them to control the velocity of their fall. Restraining both legs also prevents them from countering by stepping backward to recover their balance. You can also execute this throw by planting your R foot behind opponent's ankle, or by kicking your heel forcefully into their calf at BL-57. Hitting the chin forcefully can cause whiplash.

Defending against multiple attackers can be compared to playing chess games against several opponents simultaneously. While the principles are the same, your situation has become infinitely more complex. You must now divide your mental and physical resources among all your opponents, while each of them need concentrate only on you. It is not hard to see who is at a disadvantage. Hapkido is a composite martial art combining all the major martial technique categories. Consequently, when defending against multiple attackers you

MULTIPLE OPPONENTS

should be prepared to counter with avoiding movements, blocks, strikes, kicks, holds, chokes, joint locks, or throws—seizing any opportunity you are presented with. Some typical examples demonstrating Hapkido's unique approach to multiple opponents are shown on the following pages. Generally, there are many different opinions, tactics, and approaches for dealing with multiple attackers. The author's 1136-page Hapkido book contains 36 typical defenses, along with a comprehensive overview of basic defensive principles.

1. Against Wrist Grabs

Two attackers grab your wrists. Form Live-Hands (A). Lead your L hand forward and your R hand backward (B). Reverse direction and circle your hands in opposing directions, around attackers' wrists. Your L hand circles under and over; your R hand circles over and under (C). As your wrists lever free, grip attackers' wrists and twist their arms (D). Apply an Elbow Arm Bar to left-attacker, locking their elbow with your elbow. At the same time, apply a Scoop Wrist Lock to right-attacker, by twisting their wrist forward and up (E–F).

2. Attacking First

Step forward with your L foot. Grab the R hand of left-opponent, with your L hand (A–B). Twist their palm up, lock their wrist backward. Your palm is on the back of their hand. Grip four fingers with your R hand. Lock the finger joints and wrist by levering their fingertips toward the back of their hand. Your palm pushes fingers; your fingers pull the base joints (C). Deliver a Reverse Roundhouse Toe Kick to the groin (D). Use the pain of the hold to throw left-opponent into right-opponent (E). If they try to rise, execute a Stamp Kick to clash their heads (F).

3. Three Opponents

Three attackers are in front and on sides. Center-attacker steps forward and grabs your lapel (A). Trap their hand on your chest, gripping their wrist with both hands. Twist their arm and pull it straight (B). Pivot left and break their elbow by driving your elbow down into the joint. At the same time, deliver a R Side Kick to right-attacker, as they charge and punch (C). Left-attacker delivers a Side Kick. Step to your left and execute an Outside Wrap Block (D). Lift their leg as you step closer by shuffling your feet. Reap their support-leg with your R leg (E–F).

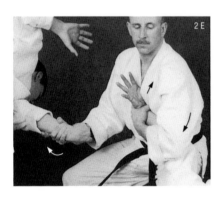
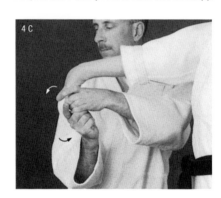

5 A   B   C

D   E   F

6 A   B   C (Elbow Arm Bar + Side Kick)

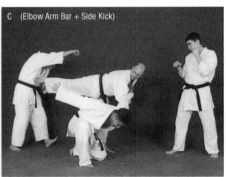

D   E (Leg Outer Reap Throw)   F

Overview

Most confrontations involving weapons generally fall into three basic categories:

- Unarmed defense against weapons
- Armed defense against unarmed attacker
- Weapons against weapons

In the author's 1136-page Hapkido book, weapons techniques are presented in separate chapters, each covering a specific class of weapons. In the larger work, more than 200 pages document over 470 weapon techniques. Since this is an introductory book, and weapons techniques are not studied until black belt level, the following six pages will provide a very brief overview of Hapkido's approach to weapons training as a whole. This will give the reader a general idea of what awaits them in later training, and show how basic principles are applied to weapons.

Historical Development

In the Asian martial arts, there are many different types of weapons, which are studied for a wide variety of purposes. Some of these weapons are obsolete and are studied purely for their historic, artistic, or spiritual qualities. Other weapons are still valued as highly effective tools for modern self-defense. Most weapons observed today are not unique to any particular martial art, but originated within Asian culture as a whole.

Historically, most Asian weaponry developed from three primary sources: the military, religious monasteries, and common citizens. Consequently, the specific characteristics of a weapon, and its uses, will often reflect these historical roots and the needs of the classes that developed them. For example, the sword is clearly a military weapon developed for warfare. In contrast, the cane is a utilitarian device, which also evolved into a potent tool for self-defense, since monks and common people were often forbidden to carry weapons. For the most part, military techniques tended to focus on the "quick kill." Martial skills developed by monks, while equally effective, tended to be more humane.

Hapkido emerged in the mid-twentieth century, hundreds of years after the development of most traditional weapons systems. Consequently, like most modern martial arts, Hapkido did not create wholly new weapons systems. Rather, it selectively adopted and synthesized those techniques from existing systems that were most in keeping with its philosophical approach to weapons and self-defense. Over the years, these techniques were further refined and modified, as various Hapkido pioneers added their own unique contributions. Thus, the weapons techniques practiced in Hapkido today possess a flavor and quality that is quite unique when compared to other martial arts. When observing Hapkido weapons techniques as a whole, one will note that the same principles found in its unarmed techniques are also integrated into weapons training. This includes concepts such as circular motion, constant movement, varied rhythm, redirection of force, blending with force, and control of internal energy (Ki). This makes Hapkido one of the few modern martial arts to truly integrate both armed and unarmed self-defense skills in a unique, comprehensive, and learnable system.

Hapkido Weapons

The variety of weapons studied in Hapkido is quite broad, and definitely a reflection of Hapkido's eclectic nature. Weapons studied fall into eight categories, which are listed below, in the order in which they are learned.

- Knife Techniques
- Short-Stick Techniques
- Long-Staff Techniques
- Cane Techniques
- Sword Techniques
- Rope Techniques
- Common Objects (held or thrown)
- Defense Against Handgun

Traditional Hapkido training did not originally include study of gun defenses, although today it is common to find these techniques being taught in many schools. Due to their importance, they are included in the larger book.

Hapkido's Approach

Hapkido's approach to weapons is defined by certain technical and philosophical qualities. From a technical point of view, it is all rather simple: weapons are conceptualized as an extension of your arm or body, and are based on the the same technical principles as unarmed techniques. From a philosophical point of view, Hapkido's approach to weapons can be summarized in three words: practical, versatile, and humane.

Practical: Real World Self-Defense

The weapons that are studied in Hapkido were originally selected for their practicality and relevance to a wide variety of circumstances that characterize modern life. Thus, Hapkido weapons are not fancy, elaborate, or expensive. They are simple, utilitarian, and innocuous—more reminiscent of tools than weapons. In a sense, Hapkido weapons are a reflection of the common objects found in one's daily life.

Versatile: Anything is a Weapon

In the eyes of a skilled Hapkido master, anything can become a weapon. If you become fluent in Hapkido's eight basic weapons-training categories, you will possess a range of skills that should allow you to wield almost anything as a weapon. Thus, in Hapkido training, the study of a particular weapon serves two purposes: 1) it teaches expertise with a specific weapon, and 2) it teaches fundamental principles and mechanics that can be applied to a range of similar common objects. For example, cane techniques can also be applied using an umbrella or a mid-length stick. Short-stick techniques can be applied with a rolled-up magazine, a piece of pipe, a hand tool, or anything else possessing similar physical characteristics. Thus, when studying Hapkido weapons, the specific physical characteristics of a weapon are considered of lesser importance than your ability to wield it effectively. Being dependent on a particular design or personalized weapon is not encouraged, since it limits your ability to handle any weapon you might acquire during the course of combat.

Humane: Act Responsibly

Hapkido's approach to self-defense is essentially humane. This has been discussed at length throughout this book, and also holds true for weapons. Generally, the preference is to immobilize an opponent without causing serious injury. While devastating techniques are also studied, they are only used in appropriate or life threatening circumstances. Be aware that anytime you strike someone with a weapon, you may be held legally liable for your actions—particularly if your opponent is unarmed. Just because you are morally in the right does not mean the legal system will agree. Exercise caution and prudence. A weapon can inflict very serious injuries.

Weapons Training

Hapkido weapons training is based on skills that have been previously mastered in unarmed defenses. If you have not mastered these skills, you will find it very frustrating to learn a weapon. Since weapons are capable of generating serious injury to yourself or others, training does not usually begin until a student reaches black belt level. At this point, the student should possess adequate physical and emotional self-control. If an instructor doubts a student's moral character, they should not teach this person weapons skills. If the instructor does and a student abuses this knowledge by injuring someone, the instructor is partially to blame.

Hapkido weapons training does not include the historic or ritualistic elements found in many other martial arts. Instead, training focuses on the development of specific offensive and defensive skills that can be applied to a variety of common self-defense situations. It must be realized that mastery of any weapon takes decades, and even then it is extremely difficult. Currently, there is a great deal of variation within the Hapkido community concerning which weapons are studied at which black belt rank. Historically, all weapons were learned by the time a person was promoted to 4th degree black belt. Some Hapkido federations are currently extending weapons training to higher ranks.

Hapkido Weapons

Knife Techniques

Short-Stick Techniques

Long-Staff Techniques

Cane Techniques

Sword Techniques

Rope Techniques

Common Objects (held or thrown)

Defense Against Handgun

Knife

Retreat into a Cat Stance. Execute a
Grab Block to attacker's wrist, using
both hands (A–B). Slide your R foot
forward. Step past with your L foot,
as you lock their elbow on your upper
arm (C). Pass under their arm and pivot
180°, twisting and locking their arm (D).
Drive the knife into their thigh as you
twist and lift their straight-arm,
breaking joints (E). A skilled attacker
will initiate a fall to save their arm (F).

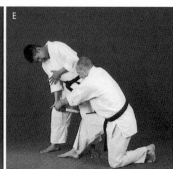

Short-Stick

Step 45° outside to avoid a R Side Kick.
Deflect and lift the ankle with your R forearm, hooking the butt around the ankle to
trap the leg (B). Drop low and execute an
Inside Snap Strike to the inner knee (SP-9
or 10) or kneecap (C). Grip the collar (D);
thrust the butt into the kidney at GB-25
(E). Step behind, pass the stick between
the legs, hook both thighs (F). Lift up
(wrist presses genitalia), as your L hand
pushes the spine, forcing a Front Fall (G).

Long-Staff

Attacker delivers a R Descending Strike or Reverse Descending Strike. From a R Defensive Stance, execute a Rising Block with your middle-section. Retract your block as you make contact, absorbing the blow's energy (A–B). Step forward to attacker's outside with your L foot. Redirect their staff downward, circling your L section forward (C). Continue rotating your staff 180° vertically, delivering a R Reverse Descending Strike to the forehead at GV-24, as your L section traps their staff (D). Using an Overhead Twirl, execute two strikes to the head in rapid sequence: deliver a L Outside Strike (E) and R Inside Strike (F).

Cane

Attacker steps forward with a R punch. Step inside with your R foot (A–B). Parry and grab their wrist with your L hand, as you deliver an Inside Strike to the ribs (C). Step in with your L foot. Pass the cane under their elbow and lock it by pressing up and back with the shaft and your inner elbow (D). Step under the arm with your R foot. Pivot 180° (arm twists) (E). Lift the wrist and press the shaft down to lock the elbow. Lever the end into the chest (F).

Press
TW-11
(elbow)

Sword

Attacker steps forward and raises their sword. As they deliver a Descending Cut, step 45° to your right with the R foot and sweep your L foot around. At the same time, execute a L Overhead Parry, striking their blade to deflect it laterally and down to your left (A–C). Continue to push their sword down, briefly trapping it (D). Turn your sword so the base of handle faces attacker (E). Thrust it into their throat or solar plexus and unbalance backward (F).

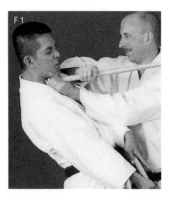

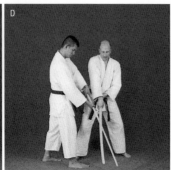

Rope

As attacker steps in with a R punch, step forward with your R foot. Deflect the blow upward using a Rising Rope Block (A–B). Circle your R hand counter-clockwise and wrap the wrist (C). As they pull their wrist away, push it into the throat (D). Circle your R hand around the neck (R to L); bind their wrist to the throat. Step behind your R foot with your L foot (E), pivot, and plant your hips low (F). Pull down, raise your hips, throw (G).

Common Objects

Once you master the principles of Hapkido's six basic weapons—short-stick, long-staff, cane, knife, sword, and rope—you will possess weapons-handling skills that can be translated to a wide variety of common objects. Thus, a letter-opener becomes a knife, a rolled-up magazine becomes a short-stick, a broomstick becomes a staff, an electrical cord becomes a rope, and so forth. Hapkido weapons training also involves study of *thrown objects*—most commonly stones, coins, plates, or darts. Typical makeshift weapons are shown at right. Many other possibilities exist.

A. Rolled-Up Magazine (rising thrust to the base of the nose)
B. Mini-Stick (pressing nerves on the wrist to initiate a throw)
C. Credit Card (slashing or gouging pressure points to release a bear-hug)
D. Throwing a stone from the ground

Defense Against Handgun

Do not try to take away a gun unless you have had qualified instruction, practice regularly under realistic conditions, and you believe there is a strong possibility that you are going to be shot or killed. In this example, the defender steps out of the line of fire, deflects and grips the gun, and then locks the gunman's wrist. After forcing a fall, the defender takes control of the handgun and pins his attacker, applying a choke with his knee.

PROMOTION REQUIREMENTS

Summary

Expertise in specific technical areas is required for promotion to specific Hapkido black belt ranks. Typical promotion requirements are summarized opposite, and expanded upon in the author's 1136-page Hapkido book. Be aware that these requirements vary widely by federation and school.

The promotion requirements given in this appendix are not intended to be an "official" document, but rather a listing of common practices. Taken as a whole, this list can be used as a model which indicates the scope and quantity of techniques that define the art of Hapkido.

The numbers in parentheses refer to the number of techniques typically required for promotion. The exact number is not important. When reviewing the listing as a whole, however, numbers will indicate the relative importance of a particular category, and the total number of techniques associated with each rank. Today many schools are reducing the total number of tech-niques in each category in order to adapt to the busy lifestyle of modern students, who have less time to train. Whether this is a wise practice is a subject of considerable debate.

Generally, over 1200 techniques are required through 4th degree black belt. The author's 1136-page Hapkido book contains more than 2000 techniques, and there are still many more.

1st Degree Black Belt
Basic Knowledge
Single Kicks (28 or 50)
Combination Kicks (30)
Ground Kicks (10)
Ground Combination Kicks (6)
Jump Kicks (13)
Defense Against Punches (40)
Defense Against Kicks (22)
Defense Against Holds (88)
Defense Against Throws (20)
Attacking Techniques (25)
Knife Techniques (69)

Total Techniques: 373 ±

(Note: All colored-belt techniques are included in the listing for first-degree black belt.)

2nd Degree Black Belt
Defense Against Punches (25)
Defense Against Kicks (26)
Defense Against Holds (74)
Defense Against Chokes (26)
Ground Defenses (38 or 54)
Defense Using One or No Arms (36)
Attacking Techniques (25)
Jump Kicks (10)
Jump Twin Kicks (6)
Jump Combination Kicks (22)

Total Techniques: 304 ±

3rd Degree Black
Defense Against Joint Locks (40)
Defense Against Throws (20)
Short-Stick Techniques (80)
Long-Staff Techniques (94)

Total Techniques: 234 ±

4th Degree Black Belt
Mastery of 1st–3rd Degree Black Belt skills
Techniques Using Attacker's Force (14)
Defense Against Multiple Opponents (36)
Protecting Another Person (7)
Cane Techniques (82)
Sword Techniques (53)
Rope Techniques (45)
Advanced Knife Techniques (37)
Defense Against Handgun (16)
Common Objects as Weapons (52)
    (common objects, mini-stick, sand, coin, stone, plate, needle, dart)
Pressure-Point Fighting
Healing Techniques (8)
Meditation and Breathing (19)

Total Techniques: 369 ±

Grand Total: Over 1200 Techniques

5th to 9th Degree Black Belt
Depending on the system, skill testing usually ends at 4th degree black belt, after which promotion is based on continued mastery of technical skills, years of service, and contributions to the art of Hapkido. Note that some Hapkido federations have extended skills testing to seventh or eighth degree. This is usually accomplished by reorganizing the same number of techniques, but over a greater number of black belt ranks (e.g., 1st–7th, instead of 1st–4th).

Hapkido Ranks

Rank [1]	Korean Name	Belt Color [1]	Min. Term [2]	Total Training	Total Hours [2]
11th Grade	11th Küp	White	2 months	none	0 hours
10th Grade	10th Küp	Yellow	2 months	2 months	120 hours
9th Grade	9th Küp	Yellow with stripe	2 months	4 months	240 hours
8th Grade	8th Küp	Green or Purple	2 months	6 months	360 hours
7th Grade	7th Küp	Green or Purple with stripe	2 months	8 months	480 hours
6th Grade	6th Küp	Blue	2 months	10 months	600 hours
5th Grade	5th Küp	Blue with stripe	2 months	1 year	720 hours
4th Grade	4th Küp	Red	2 months	14 months	840 hours
3rd Grade	3rd Küp	Red with stripe	2 months	16 months	960 hours
2nd Grade	2nd Küp	Brown	2 months	18 months	1080 hours
1st Grade	1st Küp	Brown with stripe	4 months	20 months	1320 hours
1st Degree	Cho Dan	Black	1 year	2 years	1440 hours
2nd Degree	I Dan	Black	2 years	3 years	2160 hours
3rd Degree	Sam Dan	Black	3 years	5 years	3600 hours
4th Degree	Sa Dan	Black	4 years	8 years	5760 hours
5th Degree	O Dan	Black	5 years	12 years	8640 hours
6th Degree	Yuk Dan	Black	6 years	17 years	12,240 hours
7th Degree	Ch'il Dan	Black	7 years	23 years	16,560 hours
8th Degree	P'al Dan	Black	8 years	30 years	21,600 hours
9th Degree	Ku Dan	Black; or Red with Black Stripe	9 years	38 years	27,360 hours
10th Degree	Ship Dan	Black; White; or Red with Black Stripe			

1) Hapkido originally only used white belts and brown belts, to designate ranks below black belt. Color-belt systems currently in use vary widely.

2) Minimum Term is the minimum time which must be spent at a given rank, before promotion to next higher rank. All time values given in this chart are based on 60 hours of training time per month. Thus, training for an hour per week for 2 years, is not the same as 15 hours per week for 2 years. In the United States, the average training time to 1st Degree Black Belt is about 4 years.

VOWELS

Simple Vowels

Korean Letter		Romanization	English Sound
ㅏ	아	a	as **ah**
ㅓ	어	ŏ (eo)	as h**u**t
ㅗ	오	o	as **oh**
ㅜ	우	u	as d**o**
ㅡ	으	ŭ (eu)	as tak**e**n
ㅣ	이	i	as **i**nk
ㅐ	애	ae	as h**a**nd
ㅔ	에	e	as m**e**t
ㅚ	외	oe	as K**ö**ln

Compound Vowels

Korean Letter		Romanization	English Sound
ㅑ	야	ya	as **ya**rd
ㅕ	여	yŏ	as **ye**arn
ㅛ	요	yo	as **yo**ke
ㅠ	유	yu	as **you**
ㅒ	애	yae	as **ya**m
ㅖ	예	ye	as **ye**s
ㅟ	위	wi	as **wi**eld
ㅢ	의	ŭi	as tak**e**n + **we**
ㅘ	와	wa	as **wa**nd
ㅙ	왜	wae	as **wa**g
ㅝ	워	wŏ	as **wo**n
ㅞ	웨	we	as **we**t

CONSONANTS

Simple Consonants

Korean Letter	Romanization	English Sound
ㄱ	k (g)	as **k**ing or g**r**ocer
ㄴ	n	as **n**ame
ㄷ	t (d)	as **t**oy or **d**epend
ㄹ	r (l)	as **r**ain or **l**illy
ㅁ	m	as **m**other
ㅂ	p (b)	as **p**in or **b**ook
ㅅ	s (sh)	as **s**peech
ㅇ	ng	as **ah** or ki**ng**
ㅈ	ch (j)	as **J**ohn
ㅊ	ch'	as **ch**urch
ㅋ	k'	as **k**ite
ㅌ	t'	as **t**ank
ㅍ	p'	as **p**ump
ㅎ	h	as **h**igh

Double Consonants

Korean Letter	Romanization	English Sound
ㄲ	kk	as **sk**y or Ja**ck**
ㄸ	tt	as **st**ay
ㅃ	pp	as **sp**y
ㅆ	ss	as e**ss**ential
ㅉ	tch	as **j**oy

Note: This appendix uses the McCune-Reischauer system of romanization, which is widely used in Korea and elsewhere. Bold letters within the English pronunciation examples above, indicate the portion of the word which sounds like the Korean letter.

Basic Terms

Uniform	To-bok
Martial Art School	To-jang
National Flag	Kuk-ki
Korea	Han-guk
Instructor	Sa-bŏm
Instructor, Sir	Sa-bŏm-nim
Master	Kwan-jang
Master, Sir	Kwan-jang-nim
Grandmaster	Kuk-sa
Grandmaster, sir	Kuk-sa-nim
Inheritor	To-ju ("leader of the way")
Inheritor, Sir	To-ju-nim
Founder	Ch'ang-nip-cha
Thank you	Kam-sa ham-ni-da
Hello	An-nyŏng ha-shim-ni-kka
Goodbye (to person leaving)	An-nyŏng hi ka-ship-si-yo
Goodbye (to person staying)	An-nyŏng hi kye-ship-si-yo
Art, Method	Sul
Martial Arts	Mu-sul
Way of Martial Arts	Mu-Do
Warrior	Mu-sa
Peace	P'yŏng-hwa
Self-Defense	Ho-shin
Competition (sport)	Shi-hap
Energy-Harmonizing	Ki-hap
Energy-Shout	Ki-hap
External Power	Wae-gi
Internal Power	Nae-gi
Body (physical)	Shin-ch'e / Mom
Mind	Ma-ŭm
Spirit	Chŏng-shin
Philosophy	Ch'ŏl-hak

Training Commands

Attention	Ch'a-ryŏt
Bow to Flags	Kuk-ki e Kyŏng-nye
Kneeling Position	Chŏng-jwa
Meditation	Mong-nyŏm
Return	Pa-ro
Bow	Kyŏng-nye
Relax	Shwi-ŏ
Dismiss	Hae-san

Counting	*Native-Korean*	*Sino-Korean*
One	Ha-na	il
Two	Tu(l)	i
Three	Se(t)	Sam
Four	Ne(t)	Sa
Five	Ta-sŏt	O
Six	Yo-sŏt	Yuk
Seven	il-gop	Ch'il
Eight	Yŏ-dŏl	P'al
Nine	A-hop	Ku
Ten	Yŏl	Ship

KOREAN TERMS

Stances

Stance	Cha-se
Relaxed Stance	Cha-yŏn Cha-se
Fighting Stance	Kyŏ-rum Cha-se
Offensive Stance	Kong-gyŏk Cha-se
Defensive Stance	Pang-ŏ Cha-se
Front Stance	Ap Cha-se
Back Stance	Twi Cha-se

Techniques or Actions

Technique	Ki-sul
Basic Technique	Ki-bon Ki-sul
Self-Defense Technique	Ho-shin Sul
Form	Hyŏng / P'umse
Punch	Jji-rŭ-gi
Strike	Ch'i-gi
Hit	Ttae-ri-gi
Press	Nu-rŭ-gi
Kick	Ch'a-gi
Block	Mak-ki
Joint Lock	Kkŏkk-ki
Wrestling	Ssi-rŭm
Choke	Cho-rŭ-gi
Throw	Tŏn-ji-gi
Breakfall	Nak-pŏp
Attack	Kong-gyŏk
Counterattack	Pan-gyŏk
Defend	Pangŏ

Attack Points

Fore Fist	Chu-mŏk
Back Fist	Tŭng Ju-mŏk
Hammer Fist	Mang-ch'i Ju-mŏk
Thumb Fist	Ŏm-ji Ju-mŏk
Middle Finger Fist	Chung-ji Ju-mŏk
Index Finger Fist	In-ji Ju-mŏk
Knuckle Fist	Pyŏn Ju-mŏk
Knuckle Hand	Pyŏn Son
Knife Hand	Su-do
Ridge Hand	Yŏk Su-do
Spear Hand	Kwan-su
Two-Finger Spear Hand	I-ji Kwan-su
One-Finger Spear Hand	il-ji Kwan-su
Tiger Mouth Hand	Ho-ku Su
Palm-Heel Hand	Chang-gwŏn
Bear Hand	Kom Son
Claw Hand	Kal-k'wi Son
Back Hand	Son-dŭng
Eagle Hand	Su-ri Son
Pincer Hand	Chip-kye Son
Five-Fingertip Hand	O-ji Son-kkŭt
Wrist	Son-mok
Inner-Forearm	An P'al-ttuk
Outer-Forearm	Pa-kkat P'al-ttuk
Elbow	P'al-kkum-ch'i
Ball of Foot	Ap Ch'uk / Ap Pal-ba-dak
Heel	Twi Ch'uk / Twi-kkum-ch'i
Knife Foot	Chok-do / Pal-lal
Instep	Pal-dŭng
Arch	An Jok
Knee	Mu-rŭp
Head	Mŏ-ri

Additional Korean terms and the Korean alphabet can be found in the author's 1136-page Hapkido book.

Strikes

Specific strikes are usually designated by adding the word "strike or "punch" after the attack point. For example, a Fore Fist Punch is Chu-mŏk Jji-rŭ-gi; a Knife Hand Strike is Su-do Ch'i-gi.

Punch	Jji-rŭ-gi
Strike	Ch'i-gi
Straight Punch	Chu-mŏk Jji-rŭ-gi
Hook Punch	Tol-lyŏ Jji-rŭ-gi
Uppercut Punch	Chi Jji-rŭ-gi
Vertical Punch	Se-ro Jji-rŭ-gi
Side Punch	Yŏp Jji-rŭ-gi
Wrist Strike	Son-mok Ch'i-gi
Forearm Strike	P'al-ttuk Ch'i-gi
Elbow Strike	P'al-kkum Ch'i-gi
Head Butt	Mŏ-ri Ch'i-gi

Kicks

Kick	Ch'a-gi
Front Kick	Ap Ch'a-gi
Roundhouse Kick	Tol-lyŏ Ch'a-gi
Side Kick	Yŏp Ch'a-gi
Back Kick	Twi Ch'a-gi
Crescent Kick	Pan-dal Ch'a-gi
Axe Kick	Nae-ryŏ Ch'a-gi
Hook Kick	Twit-tol-lyŏ Ch'a-gi
Spin Kick	Tor-a Ch'a-gi
Knee Kick	Mu-rŭp Ch'a-gi
Jump Kick	Ttwi-ŏ Ch'a-gi
Twin Kick	Tu-bal Ch'a-gi
Jump Twin Kick	Ttwi-ŏ Tu-bal Ch'a-gi
Combination Kick	il-lŏ Ch'a-gi

Blocks

Block	Mak-ki
Blocking Technique	Mak-ki Sul
Inside Block	An Mak-ki
Outside Block	Pa-kkat Mak-ki
Knife Hand Block	Su-do Mak-ki

Holds

Joint Lock	Kkŏk-ki
Wrist Lock	Son-mok Kkŏk-ki
Arm Lock	P'al Kkŏk-ki
Shoulder Lock	Ŏ-kkae Kkŏk-ki
Finger Lock	Son-ga-rak Kkŏk-ki
Leg Lock	Ta-ri Kkŏk-ki
Ankle Lock	Pal-mok Kkŏk-ki
Head Lock	Mŏ-ri Kkŏk-ki
Choke	Cho-rŭ-gi

Weapons

Weapon	Mu-gi
Weapon Technique	Mu-gi Sul
Short-Stick	Tan-bong
Long-Staff	Chang-bong
Cane	Tan-jang / Chi-p'ang-i
Knife	Tan-gŏm
Sword	Kŏm
Rope	Chul / Kkŭn / Tti (belt)

Philosophy and Religion

Chan, Wing-Tsit, trans. and comp.
A Source Book in Chinese Philosophy.
Princeton NJ: Princeton University Press, 1963.

Earhart, Byron H, edit.
Religious Traditions of the World.
San Francisco: HarperCollins Publishers, 1993.

Smith, Huston.
The Illustrated World's Religions:
A Guide to Our Wisdom Traditions
San Francisco: HarperCollins Publishers, 1994.

Zimmer, Heinrich.
Philosophies of India.
Edited by Joseph Campbell.
Princeton NJ: Princeton University Press, 1969.

Medicine

Cohen, Kenneth S.
The Way of Qigong: The Art and Science
of Chinese Energy Healing.
New York: Ballantine Books, 1997.

Dox, Ida; John Melloni; and Gilbert Eisner.
The HarperCollins Illustrated Medical Dictionary.
New York: HarperCollins Publishers, 1993.

Kaptchuk, Ted J.
The Web That Has No Weaver:
Understanding Chinese Medicine.
New York: Congdon & Weed, 1983.

Maciocia, Giovanni.
The Foundations of Chinese Medicine.
London: Churchhill Livingston, 1989.

Netter, Frank H.
Atlas of Human Anatomy.
Summit NJ: Novartis Pharmaceuticals, 1989.

Tedeschi, Marc.
Essential Anatomy for Healing and Martial Arts.
New York: Weatherhill, 2000.
——. *Essential Acupoints.* (Poster)
New York: Weatherhill, 2002.

Van Alphen, Jan, and Anthony Aris, editors.
Oriental Medicine: An Illustrated Guide
to the Asian Arts of Healing.
Boston: Shambala Publications, 1997.

Martial Arts

Draeger, Donn F.
Classical Bujutsu: The Martial Arts and Ways of
Japan (Volume 1). New York: Weatherhill, 1973.
——. *Classical Budo: The Martial Arts and Ways*
of Japan (Volume 2). New York: Weatherhill, 1973.
——. *Modern Bujutsu & Budo: The Martial Arts*
and Ways of Japan (Volume 3). Weatherhill, 1974.

Draeger, Donn F., and Robert W. Smith.
Comprehensive Asian Fighting Arts.
New York: Kodansha, 1980.

Farkas, Emil, and John Corcoran.
Martial Arts: Traditions, History, People.
New York: Smith Publications, 1983.

Funakoshi, Gichin.
Karate-Do: My Way of Life.
Tokyo: Kodansha, 1975.

Haines, Bruce A.
Karate's History and Traditions.
Tokyo: Tuttle, 1968.

Kano, Jigoro.
Kodokan Judo.
Tokyo: Kodansha, 1986 (first published 1956).

Lee, Bruce.
Tao of Jeet Kune Do.
Santa Clarita, CA: Ohara Publications, 1975.

Nakayama, Masatoshi.
Dynamic Karate.
Tokyo: Kodansha, 1966.

Nelson, Randy F., edit.
The Overlook Martial Arts Reader:
Classic Writings on Philosophy and Technique.
Woodstock NY: Overlook Press, 1989.

Tedeschi, Marc.
The Art of Striking: Principles & Techniques.
New York: Weatherhill, 2002.
——. *The Art of Holding: Principles & Techniques.*
New York: Weatherhill, 2001.
——. *The Art of Throwing: Principles &*
Techniques. New York: Weatherhill, 2001.
——. *The Art of Ground Fighting: Principles &*
Techniques. New York: Weatherhill, 2002.
——. *The Art of Weapons: Armed and Unarmed*
Self-Defense. New York: Weatherhill, 2003.

Korean Martial Arts

Cho, Sihak H.
Taekwondo: Secrets of Korean Karate.
Tokyo: Tuttle, 1968.

Choi, Hong-Hi.
Encyclopedia of Taekwon-do. (15 volumes)
Canada: International Taekwon-Do
Federation, 1985.

Hwang, Kee.
Tang Soo Do (Soo Bahk Do).
South Korea: Sung Moon Sa, 1978.

Kimm, He-Young.
Hapkido 2.
Baton Rouge, LA: Andrew Jackson College Press,
1994.

Lee, Joo-Bang.
The Ancient Martial Art of Hwarangdo. (3 volumes)
Burbank CA: Ohara Publications, 1978.

Myung, Kwang-Sik, and Jong-Taek Kim.
Hapkido. (Korean language)
South Korea: 1967.

Suh, In Hyuk, and Jane Hallander.
The Fighting Weapons of Korean Martial Arts.
Burbank CA: Unique Publications, 1988.

Tedeschi, Marc.
Hapkido: Traditions, Philosophy, Technique.
New York: Weatherhill, 2000.
——. *Taekwondo: Traditions, Philosophy,*
Technique. New York: Weatherhill, 2003.
——. *Taekwondo: Complete WTF Forms.*
New York: Weatherhill, 2004.

Korean Art and Culture

McKillop, Beth.
Korean Art and Design.
New York: HarperCollins, 1992.

Storey, Robert.
Korea.
Australia: Lonely Planet, 1997.

Youngsook, Pak, edit.
Arts of Korea.
New York: Metropolitan Museum of Art, 1998.

PRAISE FOR THE 1136-PAGE
Hapkido: Traditions, Philosophy, Technique

"This book is in my experience the most comprehensive ever written on a single martial art. It is superbly organized, highly informative, and contains thousands of outstanding photographs. An authoritative presentation of basic principles and techniques, integrated with modern innovations, makes this work indispensable to martial artists of virtually any style."
— PROFESSOR WALLY JAY

"Within minutes of opening Marc Tedeschi's new book, *Hapkido*, you know you have your hands on an exceptional work. *Hapkido* is an enormous, comprehensive, detailed, beautifully illustrated and, somehow, very personal reference work for those who want to learn about this fascinating martial art. I predict it will soon be as much a part of the required-reading list for martial arts practitioners as are Donn Draeger's *The Martial Arts and Ways of Japan*, Eugen Herrigel's *Zen in the Art of Archery*, and Bruce Lee's *The Tao of Jeet Kune Do*. At the same time, Hapkido goes far above and beyond these books, and beyond almost any other martial arts reference work, by examining the traditions, philosophy, and techniques of hapkido with an astonishing degree of detail . . . It covers so much ground and its material is so well presented that no martial arts library will again be complete without it."
— JOURNAL OF ASIAN MARTIAL ARTS

"If you hold this book in your hand, words will fail you. 1136 pages, more than 9000 photos, 2.5 inches thick, 11 x 8.5 inches large, and almost 8 lbs heavy! If you turn to the first pages you are lost. You forget the time and you are lost in the apparently infinite information explosion contained in this work . . . for the Hapkidoin it is a treasure chest full of information and impulses . . . If I had the choice to take a book with me onto a lonely island, I would decide on this book . . . An absolute must for any Hapkidoin!"
— HAPKIDOSHOP.COM

"*Hapkido* is an overwhelming achievement. Its comprehensiveness and the quality of the writing and design are unmatched in martial arts literature. The author's integration of history, philosophy, and technique into the larger framework of martial arts as a whole makes this book invaluable to any martial artist. Tedeschi's treatment of weapons techniques is honest, practical, and well worth studying."
— NICKLAUS SUINO, author of *The Art of Japanese Swordsmanship*

☆☆☆☆☆ *An Encyclopedia of Hapkido and Martial Arts*
"This book is simply outstanding. The depth and volume of information provided is impressive to say the least. Presented in large format on quality paper, it covers the width and breadth of Hapkido. The overview contains interviews with all prominent grandmasters, including Yong-Sul Choi. An exhaustive list of techniques are illustrated with sequence photos and detailed descriptions. It covers everything from the basics to weapons and protecting others. As a bonus, it includes extensive acupressure diagrams and descriptions. It treats Hapkido as a science without losing its art form."
— AMAZON.COM CUSTOMER REVIEW

"I am impressed. This book is one extremely large, very nearly complete, reference on all aspects of Hapkido. I say "very nearly" not as a criticism, but in astonishment, simply because this book covers almost all of a huge curriculum. In addition to a huge technique reference section, it contains a number of interesting interviews, cool historical pictures, and a number of well-written chapters on many aspects of Hapkido not normally written about . . . the verbal [technical] descriptions are the best."
— NEBRASKA HAPKIDO ASSOCIATION BOOKSTORE

"Without a doubt the best works on martial arts today are those written by Marc Tedeschi . . . great reference for anyone who is serious about learning or teaching the martial arts."
— PROFESSOR WILLY CAHILL, Two-time Olympic Judo Coach

Hapkido

Designed and illustrated by Marc Tedeschi.
Principal photography by Shelley Firth and Frank Deras.
Creative consultation by Michele Wetherbee.
Editorial supervision by Thomas Tedeschi.
Editorial consultation by Ray Furse.
Korean language services by Patrick Chew.
Production consultation by Bill Rose.
The following individuals appeared with the
author in the photographs: Arnold Dungo,
Cody Aguirre, Michael Mar, and Jo-An Aguirre.
The majority of the photographs were shot on
Plus-X Professional 2 1/4 film using Hasselblad cameras,
and were scanned from Ilford Multigrade prints
using an Epson ES-1200C flat-bed scanner.
Digital-type composition and page layout originated
on an Apple Macintosh 8500 computer.
Typeset in Helvetica Neue, Univers,
Sabon, Weiss, Times, and Futura.
Originally published May 2001 in a high-quality
softcover edition by Weatherhill,
an imprint of Shambhala Publications.
This softcover edition published May 2015
by Floating World Editions.

Floating World Editions

Printed in Great Britain
by Amazon